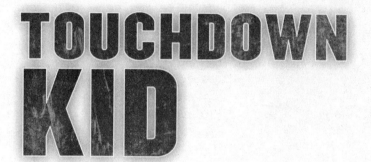

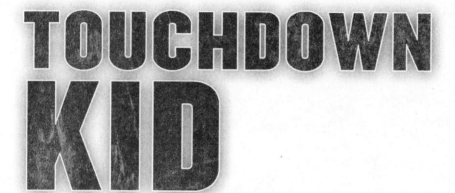

TOUCHDOWN KID

TIM GREEN

HARPER
An Imprint of HarperCollinsPublishers

Library of Congress Control Number 2017938991
ISBN 978-0-06-229385-5

Typography by Kate Engbring
17 18 19 20 21   PC/LSCH   10 9 8 7 6 5 4 3 2 1
❖
First Edition

Summer sunshine baked the blacktop in the street.

Like his best friend, Liam O'Donnell, Cory wore only his football pants, socks, and cleats. Sweat drizzled down their bare twelve-year-old chests. Vents on the roof of the corner market whined, coughing hot air so the coolers inside worked, the ice pops didn't melt, and the soda stayed frosty cold.

It was a long walk uphill to Glenwood Park. Helmets and shoulder pads had been tucked inside practice jerseys that were twisted at the belly and slung across their backs, acting like small sacks. Cory secretly eyed his friend's bare chest. Liam was like a small tank, with the compact muscles of a weight lifter bulging from skin tanned by a shirtless summer. Despite his training, Cory was short of a six-pack. The sheen of sweat on his body reminded him of the walrus at the zoo.

"Wish Coach Mellon didn't decide who starts Saturday

based on looks," Cory said, only half-kidding.

Liam flexed his arm, showing a bulge Cory could only dream of. "Pretty, right?"

Cory snorted.

"How do you know I'll start?"

"You will." Cory kicked a stone. "Mellon-head loves you."

"He might love *you* if you didn't argue with him all the time." Liam gave Cory's shoulder a soft punch.

"I can't help it." Cory knew his friend was right. Just two days ago he'd gotten into it with their coach. "An outside sweep is a thirty-eight or a forty-eight. A thirty-six is off-tackle whether there's a tight end or not."

"He's our coach, Cory."

"And it's not smart to make players go through an entire practice without water. That 'old-school' stuff doesn't cut it with me. Everyone knows you maximize performance by staying hydrated. Even a Mellon-head should know that."

Liam patted his back. "You gotta relax. Save all that smart stuff for the courtroom, when you're a real lawyer."

"I'll try."

Liam's family had moved into the poor Irish neighborhood on the city's west side at the very end of fifth grade. Most people didn't know Liam as well as Cory did, and they sometimes mistook him for a high schooler.

Cory knew different. Liam was just a silly kid like most of the rest heading into sixth grade. The world, their neighborhood, and even his older brother's belt slipped past Liam like butter off a hot knife. Liam just let it all go, looking out on it all with that big grin and always finding something funny about things, even the welts that made Cory wince.

"I'll go into the army one day. I'll go straight to sergeant with these stripes," he said once, grinning and pointing to the raised strips of skin on his left arm. "No Private O'Donnell for me."

So when they rounded the street corner and saw Liam's older brother, Finn, with some friends cluttered around the metal back door of the Shamrock Club, Liam grinned and waved while Cory looked down at the laces on his cleats. And when Liam's older brother motioned for them to come close and be quiet, Cory tried to grab his friend by the arm, but it was too late.

Liam veered right off the sidewalk and over the crumbs of broken pavement and glass, trying to look easy.

The whole thing said trouble in a million different ways.

More than the stench of the Dumpster told Cory to just run without looking back, but that would have meant leaving Liam behind. Coach Mellon would make the whole team run till they barfed if Cory showed up to a Saturday morning practice without Liam. They had a big game Sunday, and Liam was their star player. Coach Mellon said teammates had to look out for one another. They were a football family.

More than that, though, tomorrow was going to be the turning point in Liam's life. Everyone knew the HBS varsity head coach was coming to the game, and everyone knew what it could mean for Liam. Cory and Liam shared the same dream: high school superstars and Division I all-Americans, all leading to the NFL. Getting a scholarship to attend HBS, Howard Bissinger School, the elite private school known for its football program, was a big first step.

Liam had already been to visit HBS and even met the people he'd be living with. All scholarship kids had a host family. He just needed this last good game to seal the deal.

Liam was the only one who didn't seem all that excited. Why else would he even *think* about stopping for some trouble on his way to practice? Cory cared, though. He cared for Liam, and then there was the tiniest little gem of an idea sparkling in the corner of his mind that tomorrow's game could mean something for him as well.

So Cory followed, studying the situation without letting Liam's brother or his friends catch his eye.

Finn was an older, elongated version of Liam. His face had the same features—but he was always scowling. His muscles were taut, like his little brother's, only stretched out over a six-foot-three frame. Nearly a foot taller than Liam, he didn't have to work to be menacing.

Finn's friend Hoagie was as wide as he was tall, but he wasn't named after a sandwich. His last name was Hogan. His pants were hanging halfway down his wide butt and he looked not only mean but stupid, with droopy brown eyes.

And then there was Dirty. Any one of the three boys could give Cory bad dreams with just a look, but Dirty had a special stink of evil. The oldest and shortest in the bunch, Dirty had small, beetle-black eyes with a nasty, scrunched-up face. His long, dirty-blond hair hung like a curtain, covering one eye. He'd twitch his neck like a horse shooing a fly whenever he wanted to see the world with two eyes.

Dirty flicked his cigarette onto the ground and then slipped a piece of rebar—a long, rusty piece of steel that looked like a giant pretzel rod—into a padlock on the back door of the Shamrock Club. He yanked it down, snapping the lock, before he handed the rebar to Liam. "Wow. You broke it open, Liam." He looked at Cory. "You an' your friend Flapjack better keep an eye out while we get some stuff inside that needs gettin'."

Cory got called "Flapjack" because he'd eaten too much at the church pancake breakfast two years ago and got sick on Father Haywood's shoes.

"You keep watch." Finn shot Liam a meaningful look.

Liam swallowed and nodded fast. "Okay."

The older boys all laughed and disappeared inside quick as smoke.

"We shouldn't do this," Cory whispered as he watched the semi-closed door while Liam watched the sidewalk and the street.

"They won't be long." Liam giggled. "You see their faces? Hoagie looked like he's about to pee his pants. Besides, I don't need any stripes on my backside before the big game tomorrow. Guess that's how the old man did it before he skipped town. Finn doesn't want me growing up the wrong way."

Liam laughed, but it was a laugh muddy with pain.

They waited, watching. After five long minutes, Cory said, "You go to practice. I'll watch."

"Where I come from you don't just leave a friend behind." Liam sounded insulted.

"Just go." Cory sighed. "Coach doesn't care if I'm there or not."

"Don't say that. He doesn't like you, but he knows how good you are," Liam said. "Heck, you're as good as me."

"You think that?" Cory's jaw dropped. He believed he had talent—talent his grumpy coach didn't appreciate—and he'd been working hard. But even he didn't believe he'd reached Liam's level.

"Well, almost as good." Liam kissed his biceps and laughed. "Let's shoot for it. We'll let fate decide."

Liam started pumping his fist up and down. "Rock, paper, scissors . . ."

"Shoot." Cory held out a flat hand to Liam's scissors. "Scissors cuts paper. Get going."

"Okay, but you better watch good." Liam handed him the rebar, a tone of warning in his voice. "I'm serious about the butt-whipping if someone isn't on lookout when he comes back."

Cory snatched the rebar. "I never messed you up before, did I?"

"That's why you're my best friend." Liam grinned and took off in a jog toward Glenwood Park, where they practiced three nights a week and on Saturday mornings.

Too much time went by before Cory crept back to the door. He strained to hear the sound of ransacking inside the Shamrock Club's kitchen. All he heard was the walk-in refrigerator straining against the heat.

"Finn?" He said it softly first, then louder before pushing the door open and stepping over the rotted threshold.

Through the club, past the bar he could see the front door. It hung open with hot sunlight forcing its way in. Cory felt both relieved that his job was over and annoyed that they'd left him waiting like that.

7

He thought of Coach Mellon and bolted out the back door just as an enormous figure filled it.

Cory bounced back off the policeman's iron gut, tripped, and sat down hard on the linoleum floor.

The rebar clattered into the silence as Cory looked at the police-man. He was white haired, with pale green eyes and a name tag that read THORPE. The cop eyed Cory with what might have been amusement. "You can't be fourteen."

"I'm twelve," Cory said, knowing how it all looked.

Thorpe nodded at the rebar before shaking his head. "Used to be burglary was a grown man's profession."

"I-I-I'm not," Cory said. "I didn't."

"Get up." Thorpe sounded tired and annoyed.

Cory left the rebar and stood. The policeman raised his hand and Cory flinched.

"You heard too many stories." Thorpe brushed a dust bunny off Cory's bare shoulder. "I don't hit kids, even if they are burglars."

Cory shook his head violently.

"Oh yeah? Well, someone busted this door in, and you got the rebar. I'm no Sherlock Holmes, but you don't have to be on this side of the city. If you didn't do it, you better tell me who did."

Cory closed his lips tight.

"Oh, that's a big boy. You take the fall. You and I both know you'll go in front of the family court judge and he'll slap your wrist and send you home. You might end up in counseling at school. No need to go through that. I'll let all that trouble slide, but you gotta tell me who the bad guys are." Thorpe bent down and put his hands on Cory's shoulders. "You see, my partner's a rookie. He's gonna want to go by the book. He gets excited."

"FREEZE!"

Cory and Thorpe spun around to find a second policeman with his gun drawn and pointed their way from the sunny opening on the front side of the club.

"Kenny! Put the gun down!" Thorpe glowered at his partner.

Officer Kenny marched through the doorway with both hands on his gun, now pointing it at the floor. "They broke in through the front. I thought they might be in here, still."

"They broke *out* the front, Kenny." Thorpe nudged the rebar with the toe of his dusty black shoe.

Kenny sniffed the air. "Smells like someone peed."

"It's a Westside bar, Kenny," Thorpe said. "Let's take this kid home."

"But down to family court first, right?" Kenny turned his eyes on Cory like a cat sizing up a fat, juicy robin. "So we can book him? I heard they got room in Hillbrook."

Cory felt his throat tighten. Hillbrook was the name of the infamous juvenile detention center. It was only for the very worst kids, kids who committed violent crimes but were too young for jail. But even though it was a place for kids, it was reputed to be a horror show. When kids came back from Hillbrook, they were never quite right. Just the name sent chills down Cory's back.

"Maybe he gives up who did this and we bring him to his momma. You got a momma, kid?" Thorpe asked.

Cory nodded, thankful they didn't ask about a dad. That was too long of a story.

"Good. Now all you got to do is tell us who the real criminals are," Thorpe said.

Cory still shook his head. He was afraid of the police and of Hillbrook, and he was afraid of his mom, too—but not as afraid as he was of Dirty and Finn. He'd never tell.

Still, the policemen made a show of having Cory cover his belly by putting on his practice jersey. Then they put him in the back of their black-and-white squad car and turned on the siren. Cory hung his head and turned away as people on the sidewalks stopped to stare. The cops drove him downtown into the parking lot of the Public Safety Building. It was a stone fortress. Everyone on the Westside knew they kept the real criminals there.

The cops sat in the car, grilling him.

"You don't want us to take you in this place," Kenny said. "Just give us the names and we'll drive you home."

"Look, kid, just tell us what they looked like." Thorpe spun around in his seat. "You can do that much."

Cory remained silent.

Kenny shook his head in disgust. "You need to wise up, kid. Once you go through those doors, there's no going back."

12

"He's right," Thorpe said. "It'll be a lot better for you to tell us . . ."

Cory's silence continued to flood the inside of the police car.

"Let's book him, Thorpe." Kenny pounded a fist into his other hand.

"Wait."

Silence.

"C'mon," Kenny whined. "Let's book him."

Cory's lips remained closed, though. He knew his options, but even Hillbrook couldn't be as bad as waiting for Dirty to jump out of the shadows at some unknown moment.

Finally, Thorpe sighed and fired up the car engine.

"What're you doing?" Kenny's jaw dropped. "C'mon, Thorpe. Kid's a burglar."

Thorpe had both hands on the wheel, and he looked back at Cory before addressing his rookie partner. "Really, Kenny? You and your Hillbrook. You're gonna tell me what to do?"

"Well, no," Kenny mumbled. He sulked the whole way to Cory's house, a run-down place he and his mom rented on Hope Avenue. The policemen escorted him to the door while the neighborhood kids oohed and aahed and squealed with delight at the sight of Cory in a cop sandwich.

"Flap-jack got arrest-ed . . . Flap-jack got arrest-ed." Their singsong voices danced in the heat.

After several rings, his mom answered the door. Seeing the police, she gasped and snatched Cory to her side like a lost puppy. He wished she had clobbered him like most of the other moms on Hope Avenue would have done. Cory saw how the police looked at her bright yellow bathing suit beneath the open white dress shirt she'd taken from her last boyfriend. His mom must have been in the backyard.

"What's this?" Cory's mom was small and fragile as a bird, but life had made her tough. She glared accusingly at the police.

Thorpe huffed and rested Cory's football gear on the cracked stoop. "He was involved in a burglary, ma'am."

"A *what*?" Cory's mom stiffened, and her grip on his arm tightened.

Cory winced. "I didn't, Mom. Some big kids made me be the lookout. I didn't have a choice."

"Why don't you go catch *them*?" She turned her glare back at the police.

"We may have some more questions for him, ma'am." Officer Kenny tore his eyes loose from the yellow bathing suit and had a sudden interest in his belt buckle.

Thorpe had no problem meeting Cory's mom's stare and matching it with his unblinking pale green eyes. "We could have charged him with criminal trespassing and burglary third, but my sense is that he wasn't the mastermind in all this. He was there, but I'm not sure he had any intent to commit a crime."

Cory's mom frowned. "Of course he didn't."

"Well . . ." Thorpe tipped his hat and turned to go.

Cory watched them leave amid hooting and giggling from the younger neighborhood kids who had spilled back into the street. He saw the sad, knowing head wags of the adult neighbors tucked away on their front porches, hiding from the sun.

Cory's mom disappeared into the house without a word. He followed her on through, past the broken wall exposing wooden beams hammered together a hundred years ago, over the yellowed linoleum peeling up from the floor, and into the kitchen. The back door sagged open and Cory saw her empty lounge chair, her iced tea and magazine on a makeshift table. She loved sunbathing in the privacy of that wretched yard. Now she looked at him sadly. "I know you didn't do it," she said. "But how could you let yourself get in that situation?"

"I'm sorry, Mom." His voice oozed with apology, and he could see she was softening. "Mom, can you drive me over to the school? I'm really late for practice. I don't think I can make it before it ends if I walk."

"Practice! Drive you!" Her anger flared. "You're lucky I'm not punishing you. If you had a father, *he'd* punish you, I can promise you that."

"I didn't do anything."

She clenched her teeth. "You were *there*, Cory. How many times do I have to tell you? You lie down with dogs, you're *gonna* get fleas. You end up in jail, you can't be a lawyer."

Cory stood his ground. "If I don't get to practice, I can't play, Mom."

"Who says you're gonna play? Actually get in the game, I mean?" It wasn't like her to be mean, but he figured she'd been stung by the sight of the police on their doorstep for all to see.

His spirits sank as she walked out of the kitchen through the back door, ignoring his request. He followed her out into the yard where she sat back down.

"I might." Cory stood as tall as he could. "The HBS coach is gonna be there, Mom. He's coming to see Liam, but what if he sees me, too? I could go to HBS. Get a scholarship. Get

15

recruited. Play pro ball and buy you a big house. A car, too. A BMW, Mom."

She snorted and lay back and closed her eyes against the sun. She chewed on her words before spitting them out. "HBS. Howard Bissinger School. I knew a girl who went there. Kate. She was a snot. Lived above Needum's Tavern, but acted like she was a princess."

Cory's stomach flipped. He needed that ride. He couldn't say whether or not he'd get a chance to play, but he had to be ready for the possibility. He knew that for certain—as certain as he knew his mother loved him infinitely and as certain as he knew his own name. Luck was when preparation met with opportunity. That was the one thing he'd learned from Mellon-head. Tomorrow could be the day that might somehow change his life.

But he had to be ready. If he didn't make it to Glenwood Park before the Cougars' practice ended, Coach Mellon would tell him to stay home tomorrow. He'd be punished for being late, but he'd be outright banned for not making it all. Cory had seen both things happen to other kids before.

"Please, Ma," he whispered. "Please."

Cory's mom took a deep breath and let it out like a leaky bike tire. "Get your pads in the car."

He raced out the front and loaded his equipment in the green Hyundai's back seat before his mom appeared in jeans with the dress shirt buttoned and the car keys jingling in her hand.

Cory waited for her to get in.

His mom started the weary engine that broke down nearly every other week. It caught and rumbled down the street. "Want to tell me who it was?"

"Uh-uh." Cory flattened a mosquito on the windshield and flicked it out the open window into the hot stream of air.

"Thought so." Cory's mom grew up a Northside girl, but she still knew the Westside rules. "It was nice of those police to let you go."

Cory said nothing to that. He knew his mom always saw the bright side of things.

Twenty minutes later, they were in Glenwood Park, where the team was going full tilt. Cory hopped out and retrieved his gear.

"Hey." His mom waved him back and puckered her lips. "Kiss."

"Mom . . . the guys."

"The guys shouldn't be lookin' at you and me. I'm your mom and I want a kiss."

Cory kissed her quickly, secretly happy, then dashed out onto the field.

Coach Mellon ignored him. Even when he had all his gear on and helmet buckled and stood close, bouncing on his toes. He was ready for action, but he couldn't catch the coach's eye.

Liam ran a sweep for fifteen yards. The Cougars' coach blasted his whistle, clapped his hands, and shouted at the offense, "That's the way you come off the ball, boys! That's the way to run a forty-six sweep."

Finally, Cory felt compelled to speak. "Sorry I'm late, Coach."

Coach Mellon raised his Cougars cap, scratched his bald head, and looked at his watch. "Liam said you'd be late. But you're not just late. You missed it entirely. Go home."

Cory felt a chill shrink his skin. "I had to help Liam's brother so he'd let Liam come to practice, Coach. I did it for the team."

Coach Mellon kept his attention straight ahead, watching his offense. He didn't offer Cory so much as a glance, but instead lowered his eyelids. "You can't miss practice. Pollack missed and he got suspended. One game. Those are the rules, Flapjack, and I'm not bending them for *you*. You're not apt to play tomorrow anyway. You know that . . . tomorrow is a tough one, and it's Liam's coming-out party."

Cory already knew Coach Mellon underestimated him as a football player. Also, more than once, Coach Mellon had told the team that Cory was an example of how people too smart for their own good weren't usually a good fit for the game of football. "Football requires obedience, boys," Coach Mellon liked to say. "It's like the army. I say 'Jump,' you say 'How high?'"

Now was not the time for Cory to jump, though. Now he needed to stick up for himself, to advocate, which meant argue why he was right, which is what good lawyers did for their clients.

"Coach, Allred came late four weeks ago." Cory was in his element now. "Practice ended five minutes after he got here and you said *he* could play because he didn't *miss* practice entirely."

Cory's mom swore he'd grow up to be a lawyer if he kept himself out of trouble, and he hoped to prove her right. Sometimes he'd search legal terms he'd heard on TV using the computer in the school library. The really interesting ones he committed to memory. Many a night, the two of them would watch *The Good Wife*, and Cory would belt out little legal truths he'd learned from previous shows and boned up on in the library.

"That's hearsay!"

"They didn't read him his rights!"

"That judge has a conflict of interest!"

When Cory was finished in the NFL, he had every intention

of becoming a lawyer. A good one. An honest one.

"That's called a precedent, Coach," he added. "Like when a court makes a ruling and says it's illegal for the police to go into someone's home without a warrant. Even if I'm not a starter like Allred, it wouldn't look right if you went back on a precedent that you already established."

Coach Mellon turned toward him now. One of the coach's dark eyes had a mind of its own and it drifted, lifeless as a shark's eye, away from Cory, but his good eye had enough intensity for two. "You think you're on that TV show *How to Get Away with Murder* or something, Flapjack? Arguing with me like a lawyer?"

"No, sir. It's just that you always say the rules are the rules, so . . ." Cory thought of Officer Thorpe's pale green eyes and kept his gaze as steady as the scary policeman's had been.

Coach Mellon became the latest adult to huff at him that morning. "Go ahead. Get in there for Rashan. He looks like he's about to pass out anyway."

"Thank you, Coach." Cory flew across the grass. The football field was heaven to him. He loved the order of it—the huddle, lining up, reading the other side and anticipating what was about to happen. Then when things really happened—sometimes what you expected, sometimes a complete surprise—either way you had to react, to run and hustle, hit or dodge or block or tackle. It was like running through a rainstorm and that thrill you got when lightning cracked and thunder boomed, sending a chill up your back.

Rashan was so thick he made Cory look like a scarecrow. Cory tapped out the duck-footed Cougar to take his spot and play some defensive scout team linebacker in the closing minutes of practice. Some kids didn't like scout team. Cory liked it all, just so long as he was out there, and he ran around like a puppy.

After the final whistle and a pep talk from Coach Mellon about the importance of tomorrow's game, Cory stripped down to his pants and began walking away alongside Liam. Before Cory could tell him the story about the police, Coach Mellon called him back.

"Uh-oh," Liam said, setting his helmet and shoulder pads down in the dusty grass beneath a tree. "I'll wait for you."

Coach Mellon's two assistants, Coach Travis and Coach Piccolo, stood with their caps pulled low and their arms folded across their chests, flanking Coach Mellon like bodyguards. Each of them had played college football up on The Hill back in the day. They were gruff, serious men, but now they looked downright grim.

"Yeah, Coach?" Cory stood as straight as he could and sucked in his gut.

"Well, Flapjack . . ." The coach leaned sideways and spit in the grass. "Don't you want to know your punishment for being late?"

"Uh, Coach?" Cory sputtered.

"You're not much of a football player. I've told you that." Coach Mellon looked at his two assistants and they nodded like it was the truth. A wave of nausea surged in Cory's stomach.

Coach Mellon sighed. "But you show up, so you've got a place on this team. We keep everyone at Glenwood Park. The Cougars are a football family, but . . . when someone in your family messes up, what happens?"

Cory slowly shook his head, trying not to provoke the coach further.

Coach Mellon's lips curled with disgust. "Punishment . . . You just lost your spot as second-string running back. You can dress for the game tomorrow, but you're third string now."

The words plunged into Cory's heart like a knife. He'd

taken great pride in working his way up the depth chart from fifth- to second-string running back. He'd done it by working out, but mostly by studying the plays and never making mistakes. A team like theirs needed two runners at least, and late in the game he'd sometimes get some action. Third string was for a kid like Reggie Mann, who lacked not only talent but effort. Reggie hadn't even touched the ball in a game last season.

Cory's mouth sagged open. He wanted to explain exactly how it had all happened this morning—with Finn and Hoagie and Dirty. How he'd sacrificed himself for the betterment of the team, taking Liam's place so their star runner could get to practice on time.

Cory raised his hand, a habit from asking lots of questions in school. "I . . ."

It was too late. The three coaches had turned their backs on him and were talking about the defensive strategy they planned to use in tomorrow's game.

Cory shook his head and shuffled back to Liam.

"Hey, bud, what happened?" Liam asked.

Cory gave him the news.

"That's a hot mess." Liam scowled at the coaches.

Cory's face twisted in pain and he tried to muffle a certain amount of sniffing as they walked. "I was thinking if I got some carries in the game . . . I know the HBS coach—"

"Coach McMahan," interrupted Liam.

"Yeah, Coach McMahan is gonna be there to see you and you're gonna get a scholarship and—"

"*Maybe* get a scholarship," Liam interrupted again. "It looks good, but I don't actually have it yet."

"The whole Westside knows you will, Liam. Heck, you've already been to meet the host family. Tomorrow is just a formality." They stepped out of the shade onto the sidewalk, and the heat wilted Cory inside and out. "And I just thought, you know, if I had a couple nice runs late in the game that I could show him something, and if not this year—I know not this year, but maybe when I'm going into high school—I'm on his radar. Then we could play at HBS together. I hear they give out scholarships to a couple kids going into ninth grade every year, too."

"Well, if I get there and do my thing?" Liam put a hand on Cory's sweaty bare shoulder. "I'm gonna tell them about my best friend. I'm gonna tell them they need the both of us if they want a state title."

Cory smiled at his friend, swelling now with affection. "You know what I really want all this for, Liam?"

"To be great. Everyone wants to be great." Liam nodded to himself.

"Yeah, that," Cory said, "but more. It's my mom, really. I mean, you've seen how great she is."

"Yeah, she's the best," Liam said. "My mom's a nag. 'Liam, put the trash out. Liam, pick up your brother's clothes. Liam, get me a beer.' Man, it never ends."

Cory hesitated a moment to create some separation between moms before he continued, "See, all I need is a chance, then I'm gonna go to the League and buy her a big house with a pool, someplace nice, and a BMW, and she won't have to work again, ever. She can just sit out by the pool and read her books and magazines and maybe even have a maid to bring her iced tea . . ."

"And in the off-season," Liam said, "maybe we could stay there, together, and train and get in shape for the upcoming season."

"And we'll make a bet—like every season—that whoever gets the most yards, then the other guy has to take us all on a vacation, like Florida or Canada or anywhere. You too. You can bring your family if you win. I'll pay."

Liam scowled and shook his head. "Not them, Cory. I want to get as far away from them as I can."

That dampened Cory's spirits a bit, but they dropped their equipment at Cory's house and headed for the park.

They spent the afternoon pushing and shoving for an open spot in the public pool at Burnett Park, leaving the water only for peanut butter and jelly sandwiches Cory's mom had wrapped in reused aluminum foil. They drank water from the fountain, even though there was a line there too. Summer in the city wasn't just hot, it was crowded.

That night, Cory and his mom watched a video borrowed from the library. Sleep came slow. Even the whirring blades of the plastic fan right next to his head brought little relief from the heat held tight inside their house after a day of baking.

When he woke, it was game day.

Nervous electric spiders crawled up and down Cory's arms and legs. Even though he didn't expect to play, Cory felt the excitement of an entire community crowding the bleachers and sidelines to watch. The Westside took pride in the toughness and speed of its teams. On the Westside, any football game—even a kids' Pop Warner team—was a serious event.

After a breakfast of Cocoa Puffs and milk, they got ready.

Cory's mom wore team colors, white and green, with her long, dark hair tied up in a ribbon to match her clothes. Cory dressed carefully, wanting to look good if nothing else. He checked himself in the mirror to do the final tuck of his jersey into the white pants. His mom appeared, and in the mirror he saw the similarities in their faces: the big brown eyes with a slightly sad tilt, small ears, and that pointy chin. But Cory's face was rounder than his mom's and his neck much shorter and thicker, which he knew came from his father.

The last time he'd seen his father, Cory had been just four, but he could still close his eyes and picture the man, standing in the doorway in his army uniform, kissing Cory's mother good-bye. He'd been a fist of a man, compact and strong, with a wide, round face, and his arms had wrapped around Cory's mom like pythons.

Cory was seven when his mother told him that his father was dead. They never talked about how he died, and Cory wasn't sure his father had actually been killed in combat in Afghanistan, even though that's the story that had grown into an accepted fact by everyone over the past four years. There was never a funeral or any other mention of his father specifically, unless Cory counted the endless times his mother referred to the punishment he'd get *if* he had a father.

Cory suspected his mom and dad were never married, which was why he shared his mom's last name. It would also explain the absence of a funeral or any kind of army money. Maybe they had a kind of star-crossed–lover thing like Romeo and Juliet.

As they pulled into Glenwood Park, Cory was shaken from

his thoughts. Two dozen cars already had the best parking spots.

"We're late," Cory said.

"You're not late," his mom said.

"If you're not early, you're late."

"Says who? It's nine twenty and the sheet says nine thirty."

"Coach Mellon, Ma." Cory launched himself out the car door.

His mom shouted after him. "Good luck!"

Cory waved a hand back over his head, dashing for the field. More than half the team was assembled, already zinging footballs back and forth. Cory's three coaches stood off to the side, behind the bench, surrounding a man who towered over them. The HBS head coach, Coach McMahan, wore a crimson-and-silver HBS Football cap that shone like a rare jewel in the sea of green and white.

Cory tried not to stare, but as he neared the sideline to drop his water bottle under the bench, he saw Coach McMahan's bright blue eyes shining right at him. Cory froze beneath the coach's gaze. The light in his eyes gave Cory a feeling of welcome, and a seed of joy burst open in his chest.

Coach McMahan pointed right at him, *him*! Cory poked a finger in his own chest, still unsure, but all that did was make Coach McMahan smile more broadly. He motioned for Cory to come over.

"Come on, Flapjack." Coach Mellon's face reddened with impatience. "Coach McMahan wants to talk to you."

Cory marched straight for the man, feeling certain that his entire life was about to change.

Up close, Coach McMahan was kind of scary. His smile was still bright, as were his blue eyes, but something in those eyes seemed to look right through Cory. He put an arm around Cory's shoulder pads and looked at Coach Mellon. "Mind if I borrow him for a few minutes so we can talk?"

"Whatever you need, Coach," Coach Mellon said obediently, reminding Cory of Liam's mutt, Alice. She was the sweetest dog Cory had ever seen, and when Liam got home from school, he'd croon to her like a baby and scratch her ears. Alice would tremble and wag and piddle right down her leg. Cory looked for a wet mark on Coach Mellon's pants and bit back a smile. Scolding himself for thinking silly things when he was on the edge of a whole new life, Cory followed the HBS coach.

"Sit down, Cory." Coach McMahan pointed to the end

of the bench, out of listening range of the entire team. Cory sat and Coach McMahan took the spot next to him. "Being admitted to HBS isn't just about sports—despite what people say. It's about academics and character, too. Those are every bit as important as athletic performance. Howard Bissinger was a philanthropist who stood for the complete man."

Coach McMahan gave Cory a look that dared him to think otherwise.

"Yes, sir," Cory said, nodding. Now it was starting to make sense. Cory was one of the top students in his school, and he had a reputation not only for following the rules but for kindness to others. His teammates were pretending not to notice that he was sitting there with the HBS coach, but he knew they couldn't keep their eyes off him. Pride crept through him, and he had to smile.

"Good." The coach clapped Cory on the back. "That's why I need you to be totally honest with me. Can you do that?"

"Yes, sir." Cory felt he might burst.

"About Liam."

Cory blinked at those blue eyes, trying to read them, but coming up with a blank page. "Sir?"

"Liam." Coach McMahan nodded out toward the middle of the field where Liam was winning some sort of tag game. "Your coaches say no one knows him better than you."

Cory heard a tremendous sucking sound in his brain, like the flush of the toilets at school where the water roared through the pipes from the pressure. Through the noise, he heard his own crumbling voice. "Yeah, Liam is great. He's the best."

"He's got a brother who's a bad egg, though?" Coach

McMahan raised an eyebrow. "Gets rough with him some-times, I hear."

Cory nodded without thinking. His brain was pudding right now. "Yes, sir."

"See, that's good." Coach McMahan gave Cory's shoulder a little shake. He was terribly strong. "You're not just feeding me gumdrops and candy canes. Does he do his homework and things like that?"

"Uh . . ." Cory didn't want to out his friend, but he felt it would be even worse to lie to this man. "He's not much on homework, but when he comes to my house after school, I have to do it, and he definitely does it with me."

Coach McMahan rubbed his chin. "Hmm, well we've got tutors for that sort of thing. As long as he's a good kid, no trou-ble, right?"

"No, sir." Cory shook his head violently, glad to be off the subject of studying. "Last week Liam found a pair of shorts at the pool with five dollars in the pocket and he brought it to the lifeguard. That's Liam."

Coach McMahan beamed at him. "You can make up for a lot of other character flaws with some good old-fashioned honesty, can't you?"

"Yes, sir."

"And no girlfriends or any of that kind of nonsense yet, huh?"

"No." Cory smiled. He and Liam had a rule—no girls before the NFL.

"No smoking, drinking, or drugs?"

"No." Cory shook his head so hard he wouldn't have been

surprised to see his ears take off like flying saucers.

"Excellent!" Coach McMahan stood up and so did Cory. "Say, why do they call you Flapjack?"

Cory sighed and looked away before he answered, his voice barely more than a whisper. "I guess sometimes I eat a little more than I should." He couldn't remember a time in his life when he'd been more embarrassed.

"Don't we all?" Coach McMahan patted his iron stomach and grinned. "Hey, good luck out there today. Go get 'em."

"Thanks, Coach." There was nothing else Cory could do besides jog off toward the gang of teammates now swarming around Coach Mellon in the end zone.

The Cicero Falcons arrived at the field, and after brief warm-ups, eleven of Glenwood Cougars' finest took the field to battle them. While Cory stewed in shame for thinking Coach McMahan might actually have had a place for him, Liam ran wild out on the field. Cory didn't know if it was because Liam knew Coach McMahan was watching, or if it was just that his stars were all lined up perfectly, but by halftime Liam had run 126 yards and scored two touchdowns. The only reason he didn't have more was because the Cougars quarterback had a serious case of the fumbles. Three times he lost the snap in the red zone before being yanked from the game and replaced by the backup quarterback late in the second quarter.

The fumbles, along with a dozen penalties, cost the team the lead. They were down 28–14, and during halftime, with the boys all sitting cross-legged on the grass in the end zone sucking on orange wedges, Coach Mellon stomped among them like an ogre. Cory wondered how much was a show for

31

Coach McMahan's benefit—Mellon wanting to impress the HBS coach with his intensity and toughness. Real or not, three kids got clunked on the head by Coach Mellon's clipboard.

Whether it was the clipboard or the yelling, the Cougars began the second half like a house on fire. Their defense forced the Falcons to punt after three plays, and then Liam led the march right back down the field. They were on the goal line ready to score when Liam ran a toss sweep to the strong side, where the defense was waiting for him.

And then it happened—almost like in a movie—all slow motion. Cory saw the hits from the defense on Liam—one high and one low—and then Liam's shriek pierced the air.

Everyone in the stands gasped at the same time, then went strangely quiet. Players from both teams backed away from the mess that had been Liam's knee only moments ago. Liam paused only to snatch a breath of his own before screaming again. Coach Mellon came unstuck from his spot on the sideline and dashed out with the other two coaches flanking him. Liam's ferocious brother vaulted the chain-link fence and beat everyone to his brother's twisted shape.

Cory swallowed to keep his Cocoa Puffs breakfast down. He knew every dream Liam had ever dreamed had just come to a quick and painful end.

The ambulance came within minutes and Liam was put on a board with his ruined leg strapped down to keep it from moving. He was loaded into the back of the ambulance that took off, siren blaring, as his teammates stood by, silent and watching helplessly.

Cory's mom always said you could never look back.

It was a saying Cory had grown tired of. Still, there it was in the front of his mind, exactly what she said you couldn't do. The moment he couldn't help looking back at was when he'd taken Liam's place outside the Shamrock Club. Had he simply gone to practice instead of Liam, as Liam suggested, things would be different. Liam would have been late and Coach Mellon might not have started him in the game as a punishment. He might even have called a different play on the goal line, something less flashy than a toss sweep to show off his speed. Maybe a run up the gut, banging and battering through a bunch of big linemen to make him really work for the touchdown.

Whatever else, even if Liam had ended up getting hurt, Cory wouldn't have been late and he wouldn't be buried in the depth chart beneath Reggie Mann. Was it wrong to think of himself? Right or wrong, he couldn't help it. Liam wasn't the only one with dreams.

Reggie Mann, now the second-string running back, took Liam's place. On the second play, Reggie got stood up at the line and coughed up yet another Cougars fumble. Four plays later, during a Falcons punt, Reggie got laid out on a blindside hit that left him teary eyed. Cory clenched his hands and tasted the rubbery flavor of his mouthpiece as Coach Mellon looked him over and walked away. Cory hovered around Reggie, who sat defeated on the bench while the Cougars defense made a stand. He wanted to tell Reggie to take it easy, that he'd be happy to go in . . .

But before he knew it, Coach Mellon appeared and barked something about needing to be tough. Reggie gave a nod, snapped up his helmet, and jogged out to the field to join the offensive huddle.

Cory's insides clenched and twisted. That could have been him, with a chance to shine.

He turned around and saw that, yes, Coach McMahan still stood at the top of the bleachers with the brim of his cap pulled low, a pencil in one hand, and a notepad in the other. Even with Liam out of the action, the HBS coach had decided to stick around. The cruelty of missing such a chance crusted Cory's heart with bitterness.

But still, hope—like summer weeds—sprang up in Cory's chest, making him tense.

The Falcons defense must have smelled blood. When Reggie ran upright through the B gap, he got slammed by the middle linebacker. People doing yard work halfway across the city probably heard the hit. Reggie dropped to the ground. Cory trembled as the coaches went out to help Reggie off the field.

Cory's fingers groped for his helmet resting beneath the bench. He fumbled with the chinstrap, buckling up, ready for action.

He took a deep breath and stepped right up to Coach Mellon, meeting his eyes.

What happened next was hard to believe.

"I'm here, Coach," Cory said.

But Coach Mellon looked past him, searching the sideline until he saw Gunnar Miller. Gunnar was only a backup wide receiver, but he was one of the fastest kids on the team. Coach Mellon brushed right past Cory and put his hands on Gunnar's shoulder pads.

"You can do this, Gunnar," Coach Mellon said. "Just take the handoff and run through the hole we call in the huddle. Two, four, six to the right, one, three, five to the left. We'll mostly run outside so you can use your speed, so seven and eight will be the big ones. Even is to the right, odd to the left."

Even Cory could see the confusion—and maybe fear—in Gunnar's eyes.

Cory tapped Coach Mellon's arm. "Coach, I . . ."

Coach Mellon brushed Cory off like a mosquito. "Not now, Flapjack, *not now!*"

Cory watched Gunnar step onto the field, dipping his toe in the turf like it was a cold pool. Coach Mellon patted him on the butt. "You can do it, Gunnar! We can win this!"

Cory glanced back into the stands. Coach McMahan was still there, but he was talking with someone, not watching the game. Cory's eyes went back out to the field, and he crept close to the coaches, standing directly in Coach Mellon's shadow.

"Give me a forty-six sweep," Coach Mellon barked at Coach Travis, who signaled the play to their quarterback.

On the snap of the ball, everyone went right, but Gunnar went left. The Cicero defense dropped him for a seven-yard loss. Coach Mellon cursed and slapped his own leg.

"He just doesn't know," Coach Travis said.

"Doesn't know right from left? Odd from even?" Coach Mellon grabbed the hat off his own head and spun around, strangling it. "Try forty-five sweep."

"You want me to just shout out to him to go left?" Coach Travis asked.

"You think the Cicero Falcons are deaf, Chuck?" Coach Mellon spun back toward the field and shook his head in disbelief.

"Right." Coach Travis turned and signaled a forty-five sweep to the quarterback.

Gunnar ran the wrong way again, losing another four yards.

Cory glanced back at the stands. Coach McMahan was watching now. Cicero's wild cheers for their defense had gotten his attention. Cory's eyes found his mom, pretty and small and cheerful, standing to clap encouragement to the team. The woman next to her jumped up to shout, nearly knocking Cory's mom over. Cory thought about the daisies his mom planted once. They were like her, sweet and delicate and pretty, surrounded by tough people from a rough neighborhood.

Pressure squeezed Cory's chest, making it hard to breathe. He knew he was asking for trouble, but still, he tapped Coach Mellon on the back of his arm until he turned around. "Flapjack, *what?*"

"Coach, I know the plays. I can do this."

Coach Mellon chewed on his lower lip, then glanced at Coach McMahan in the stands.

Coach Mellon sighed and wiped a hand over his face.

"Okay, Cory. Run a forty-two dive. Get in there."

Cory dashed toward the huddle, yelling Gunnar's name and waving for him to come off.

Too excited about his chance, he stumbled. Even from his perch at the top of the bleachers, Coach McMahan had to be able to hear the Falcons defensive players laughing. Cory dusted himself as he rose.

"Forty-two dive," he told the quarterback.

"It's third down," complained one of the linemen. "Why don't we pass?"

"Why don't you shut up?" said the quarterback.

"C'mon guys," Cory said. "Let's do this. We can win this."

The lineman rolled his eyes. "You and what army? Wait till you get blasted by these guys. You'll be crying for your momma."

Cory jammed his mouthpiece onto his upper teeth and bit

down, staring hard at the quarterback. His insides burned with fury. The quarterback rolled his eyes and called the play. They went to the line.

The ball was snapped. Cory lunged forward, taking the handoff.

The first man to hit him was the defensive tackle, unblocked. Cory blasted into him and spun. The left side of the line had collapsed. Cory bolted right, ducked under the defensive end, and found some daylight. A linebacker dove at his knees. Cory high-stepped, tearing free, got hit again, and spun again. The safety was veering toward him like a heat-seeking missile. Cory lowered his shoulder and dropped the safety before plowing over the top of him. A linebacker came at him from the other side.

Cory held up his hand like a traffic cop, jamming the palm flat into the linebacker's facemask and guiding his head into the turf before leaping over him. Then the field was wide open, nothing but a zebra—a referee—on the green. The goalpost waited for him like the gates to heaven, shiny and gold. He turned on all the speed he had.

Crossing the goal line in full stride, Cory ran right through the back of the end zone before turning to see the mess of bodies he'd left behind.

A Cougars stampede charged him. Cory laughed and let the slaps rain down on his helmet. He grinned and chuckled, smacking high fives with everyone, even the lineman who'd doubted him. Back on the sideline, Coach Mellon gave him a funny look. "That was pretty good, Flapjack. What got into you?"

Cory shrugged and forced himself not to look into the stands at Coach McMahan.

"Well . . ." Coach Mellon glanced at Coach Piccolo, who ran the defense. "Who goes in for Liam on D?"

Coach Piccolo consulted his clipboard and flipped a page. "Uhhh . . ."

"Can you play the outside backer the way you ran that forty-two dive?" Coach Mellon asked Cory.

"Yes!"

"Get in there."

After two run plays that went away from Cory, the Falcons quarterback rolled out to pass. Cory saw the tight end dragging across the field underneath the coverage. He read the quarterback's eyes and knew where it was going. It was a risk to leave the zone he was supposed to be covering, but Cory trusted his instincts.

Just as the quarterback let go of his pass, he was hit by a Cougars defender. The ball wobbled in the air. Cory darted in front of the tight end, snatched the ball, and cruised into the Cougars' end zone for another touchdown, tying the game. His teammates mobbed him, and once again he found himself standing on the sideline with a bewildered Coach Mellon as the Cougars kickoff team took the field.

"Well . . ." Coach Mellon grabbed Cory's shoulder pad and gave him a little shake as if to make sure he was real. "What play would you like to run when we get the ball back?"

Cory shrugged like it didn't matter, because he felt like he could do anything. "Sweep?"

"Okay, a forty-six . . . no, a *forty-eight* sweep." Coach Mellon nodded and laughed. "Now get out there and stop them, and then we'll get you that sweep."

Cory didn't have another spectacular play on defense, but the Cougars held, and midway through the fourth quarter, he was in the offensive huddle again. His teammates looked at him through the bars of their facemasks, eyes glazed by new-found admiration. The quarterback called a forty-eight sweep.

"You can do it, Flapjack."

"You got this, Cory."

"Make it happen, Big Dawg."

They broke the huddle with a single, confident clap. Cory lined up deep behind the quarterback and surveyed the defense. They moved like the men who sometimes left the Shamrock Club after an evening of drinking, stepping carefully one way, then the other. The defense wasn't just confused, they were worried.

Once Liam got hurt, the game was supposed to open up for them like a birthday gift—nothing but some flimsy wrapping paper to dispose of before they could enjoy their victory.

Things were different now, though, because some chunky third-stringer had just evened the score. Now here he was again, standing tall, looking them over like he'd look at a tray of donuts.

Cory put his hands on his knees, but still his eyes flickered over the defense. When the ball was snapped, he took off to the right. He saw the quarterback pivot and toss the ball on a long, slow arc that landed in his hands. Cory covered the tip with his palm and tucked it tight. Then he did his thing.

Three defenders got their hands on him. But none could bring him down.

Cory's sixty-three-yard touchdown gave them the lead. The Cougars fans went crazy.

Three times he'd touched the ball; three times he'd scored.

As he marched toward the sideline under a thumping of hands, he thought to look up into the stands.

When he did, he realized—with horror—that Coach McMahan was already gone.

While victory was sweet, the stink of disappointment fouled Cory's spirits. He'd never done anything close to what he'd done today. He wasn't sure he could ever do it again. Coach McMahan's absence was the tragedy of a lifetime.

"Why the face?" His mom had an arm draped over his shoulder. They had exhausted the congratulations of the other parents, teammates, and Westside football fans and were walking slowly toward their car.

"I did all that and he wasn't even here." Cory hung his head.

"Who?" His mom put a hand on his neck and squeezed, speaking sad and slow. "Your father?"

Cory looked up, jolted by the word. "My father?"

"I . . . I didn't know what you meant," she said. "You said 'him.'"

"I meant Coach McMahan, from HBS. He was here to see Liam, but he left."

"Oh." She hugged him tight with one arm and they stumbled along toward their car. "How do you know he left . . . that coach?"

"You can't miss him. Tall guy, silver hair. Crimson hat."

"It doesn't matter. You played great for you and your team." His mom fumbled with her keys. "Besides, I don't want you going so far anyway. HBS is a football factory. You're going to be a lawyer, Cory."

They separated, and Cory looked at her over the rusted roof of the car as she unlocked the doors. "Football can pay for college," he said. "I can go to law school *after* I play in the pros."

She burst into a smile and a gust of laughter floated up into the muggy air. "A couple touchdowns and you're already in the NFL, huh?"

A voice behind Cory said, "Nothing wrong with dreaming the dream."

The voice was low and strong. Cory saw the look of surprise on his mom's face, and he spun around.

Coach McMahan was standing there, smiling. "What'd you say your name was?"

"Flap—Cory. Cory Marco." Cory trembled with the thought of a new beginning. No more Flapjack, no more reminder of the infamous mess on Father Haywood's shoes.

"And are you Mrs. Marco?" Coach McMahan peered over the top of the car at Cory's mom, and his voice took on a different tone.

"Call me Ashley," Cory's mom said. "It's just Cory and me."

"Your son, Cory, was something out there today," Coach McMahan said. "He was like some kind of Touchdown Kid."

The coach smiled at Cory's mom, but she didn't seem to understand what he meant.

"For a while there, every time he got the ball, he scored a touchdown," Coach McMahan explained. "I'd like to talk to you both about HBS."

Cory's mom put her hands flat on the roof of the Hyundai. "Cory's going to be a lawyer."

Cory wanted to melt. His mom didn't seem to have a full measure of respect for things like the police or the head coach of a big private school. He flashed her a dirty look, hoping to slow her down. But Coach McMahan didn't seem put off. His smile got so wide Cory could see the silver fillings in back.

"That's great news," the coach said. "We've had many, many HBS graduates go on to become lawyers. HBS is one of the finest academic institutions in the state. Our rate of college enrollment is almost one hundred percent."

"Hmm," Cory's mom said before she nodded. "Keep talking."

They followed Coach McMahan's white Tahoe SUV to the Dunkin' Donuts on the corner of Velasko Drive and Grant Avenue to talk.

Dunkin' Donuts was Cory's idea of heaven.

You could get anything, and with Coach McMahan paying, that's what Cory did. He began with a turkey, bacon, and cheese croissant sandwich and a side of hash browns. To wash it down, he ordered a Strawberry Coolatta, and the girl behind the counter had no problem topping it off with extra whipped cream. Dessert was part of a balanced meal to Cory. He chose a pink-frosted glazed donut with a rainbow of sprinkles as well as an Oreo Cheesecake Square.

His mom and the coach sipped their iced coffees, watching Cory eat. Coach McMahan set his cup down on the table and said, "Fate is a fickle mistress."

Cory wasn't sure what fickle meant. It rhymed with pickle, though, and that made him grin. Fate was also something he knew he should know about, but didn't really.

"You mean Liam getting hurt?" Cory's mom asked.

Coach McMahan slowly turned his coffee cup halfway around. "I was thinking about Cory, but you're right. Liam's loss is Cory's gain."

"What do you mean? Can't both of us go to HBS?" A surge of guilt left Cory feeling panicked. "Liam too, when he's better?"

"Anything's possible," Coach McMahan said. "He could make the ninth-grade cut. But Liam's knee is in pretty bad shape—dislocated. He won't be back on the football field anytime soon. So, I started thinking right away about filling his spot with three other kids we've been looking at. Then, well . . . what I saw from you just now? That Touchdown Kid thing? I think we're both lucky. Right place, right time . . . that's fate."

"So, you want me to go to HBS?" Cory felt silly coming right out and asking, but he was giddy with the words *Touchdown Kid* ringing in his ears, and he needed to hear it.

"Yes. That's why we're here. It usually doesn't happen like this. You know I've met with Liam's mom and brother, and they've even visited the host family. They had time to absorb the whole HBS experience. It's life changing." Coach McMahan leaned halfway across the table to make his point. "Everyone there is headed to college. Preparation begins in sixth grade. Homework is something everyone does. Studying for tests. Writing papers. Reading.

"I mean, you're there to play football, too," Coach McMahan

said, leaning back with a sly smile and looking at Cory's mom. "But he'll get an education in a setting that will allow him to be whatever he wants to be. Lawyer? That's easy coming out of HBS." He paused. "I mean, look, not all public school is awful, but the opportunities for Cory after going to HBS are huge."

Cory's mom bit her lip and nodded.

"I read somewhere that some of these city high schools have a fifty-four percent graduation rate." Coach McMahan frowned and looked around at the noisy mayhem inside the restaurant. Parents were piled up in orange booths with little kids screaming and running around the tables. Then he nodded at the window. Outside, a fistful of teenagers hung around smoking. "How many of them are going to college?"

Cory's mom's face did some gymnastics before coming to rest with a small smile. "I'd love to see Cory at a private school. It's just . . . with me working two jobs, I . . . my car's not the most reliable to get him there every day."

Coach McMahan cleared his throat. "Well, a lot of our scholarship kids are in the same boat. That's why we have a host family all lined up. You see, HBS is like one big family. We take care of our own. And the football team? That's a family within a family."

"What does that mean?" Cory's mom asked.

"We have a place Cory can live, with other HBS kids." Coach McMahan opened his arms in a welcoming gesture. "A home."

Cory's mom's face soured. "Like an *orphanage*?"

Coach McMahan shook his head. "No! Not that kind of home—a *real* home. A teammate whose parents want to help.

His own bedroom . . . everything. Our scholarship kids typically end up feeling like they've got an extended family."

Cory's mom scowled. "Cory's not living with anybody but me."

"I know it might take some time to get used to the idea." Coach McMahan's face looked frozen. "Liam's mom had some reservations too, at first, but she even ended up helping decorate his new room . . ."

Still Cory's mom shook her head as she set her coffee on the table and pushed it away. "There's nothing to get used to. It's me and him. *We're* the family."

Cory saw light leave Coach McMahan's eyes. "This is a lifetime opportunity, Mrs. Marco. It might not come around again."

"Thank you for the coffee, Coach McMahan." Cory's mom wiped her mouth on a paper napkin and stood to go. "Cory's fine right where he is."

Cory had so many feelings he didn't know what to think or say. His heart felt like an ice-cream cone spilled onto the hot summer street.

"Mom, we—"

"Get in the car, Cory." His mom marched across the parking lot, guiding him by the elbow.

Cory looked back inside the Dunkin' Donuts where Coach McMahan sat sipping his coffee as if nothing unusual had occurred. Cory wondered if he'd ever had something like this happen before. He doubted it. Kids on the Westside didn't say no to HBS. They weren't thinking about law school. Their parents *wanted* them at a football factory.

Everyone on the Westside knew about Jo-Lonn Dunbar. He started out like a lot of kids with just a dream, but *he* went to HBS to play football—lived in the weight room. He went on to Boston College before signing with the Saints and winning a Super Bowl. Everyone talked about the ring and the glory and the *money*. He was a local hero. Coty had seen Jo-Lonn's dark gray Mercedes G-Wagen floating away up South Avenue like a ghost after the famous player had spoken at a fund-raiser for a city councilwoman. And, while he hadn't seen the player himself, he had seen the SUV with its glittering silver trim, so he knew it was all real.

Cory got in the little green car. He looked at her, desperate. "Mom, *please*."

His teardrops plopped onto the cloth seat.

"Really?" His mom wrinkled her face because she hated when he cried. "You're gonna do *this*? You're gonna *cry*?"

Cory sniffed. He could barely speak. Finally, he choked it out. "It's what I dreamed of, and it *happened*. It really happened, and now you're just gonna crush it? How can you do that?"

She huffed and turned the key.

The engine wound itself up, sounding old and tired before it slowed down to a steady wavering groan. She turned it off, then tried again. After a small spurt of energy, the little car moaned as if dying from pain. She turned the key and slapped the dashboard.

"Piece of *junk! Junk! Junk! Junk!*"

And then she was crying too. She grabbed the wheel and buried her face in her arms, trembling as if she were cold. Words leaked through her thick web of hair. "I don't want to lose you, Cory. And I know that's what will happen if you go to HBS. *I-I don't want to lose you.*"

Cory put a hand on her back and felt her bones buried like the blade of a shovel beneath her skin. "You're not gonna lose me, Mom. I'll be right here, I promise. I can come home every weekend and vacations and all summer. We can do all the stuff we do, cookouts and movies and the mall. And you work so much anyway. Half the nights I don't even see you."

"I know, but I do it all for you, Cory. So we can have a decent life." As bad as Cory felt for his mom, his eyes couldn't help but track the path of Coach McMahan as he left the donut shop. The big man cruised across the parking lot, head tilted down beneath the low brim of his hat, checking his phone. Cory felt a spark of urgency. "But this would give me so much, Mom. Look, the coach is leaving. You've got to stop him so I can go." He paused. "Please?"

With a cackling sound that was part sob and part crazy laugh, his mom sprang from the car and dashed across the parking lot just as Coach McMahan pulled open the wide door of his big white SUV. Cory clenched his hands and watched them talk.

When his mom reached up and hugged the coach, Cory let go of a breath he didn't even realize he'd been holding.

Cory spent the next day at the rec center at Burnett Park marking time until he could see Liam at the hospital where he'd had surgery after the game. When his mom returned from work, she picked him up so they could shower and change their clothes before driving to see Liam. At the hospital, his family waited in the lounge area. Aunts, uncles, and cousins all were there, downcast and hushed.

Liam's brother scowled when he saw Cory. Liam's mother whispered hello and then escorted them into the hospital room, sniffing and sobbing as she went. Her hair was a messy nest and smelled like smoke. Cory and his mom pushed past the tangle of balloons and flowers to find Liam with his leg suspended from the ceiling and wrapped tight like a mummy's. His face was puffy, and when he opened his eyes just a slit, they were wet and shiny.

Liam forced a smile and raised a weary hand trailing an IV tube. "Hey, Cory."

"Hey, Liam." Cory bit his lip, afraid he might break down. He had never imagined Liam so weak.

"They hit me good, but I guess they say they got it fixed." Liam's eyes rolled up in his head, and he closed them.

"What are *you* doing here?" Finn entered the room and put his tattooed hands on the end of the bed, leaning toward them and sticking out his lower lip.

Cory looked at his mom. She put her hands on her hips, unafraid. "We are here to see how Liam is doing."

"Because you gonna take his free ride to HBS. You're feelin' bad, huh?" Finn was snarling now. "Yeah, I'd feel bad too. You want to feel good about it? You want to think like the best man won? Well, the best man is Liam. Nothing is going to change that."

"Finn, please," his mom said.

Cory's mom cleared her throat. "The way I understand it, Finn, there may be an opportunity for Liam later."

"Except all of a sudden Coach McMahan won't return my texts." Finn pointed at an enormous arrangement of flowers, the biggest bunch by far. "See that? Says, 'Good luck. So sorry things didn't work out.' From the Muillers, the people—I'm guessing by your clothes—you're about to go meet. HBS snobs. You believe what you want to believe, but I know you're takin' Liam's spot, and I'm asking you to leave, now."

"Liam? I—" Cory started, but Liam just turned his head.

"See ya, Cory," he whispered. Liam's mother nodded, silently agreeing that they should go.

Cory's mom had a fire in her eyes. "Well, no good deed goes unpunished. Come on, Cory, let's go."

They climbed into his mom's car and rode in silence, up onto the highway and out toward the suburbs where most of the people whose kids attended HBS lived. The car trembled and whined like a stray dog. Hot air waffled in and out through the open windows. Cory's mom struck the steering wheel with her hand and spoke as if someone had asked her a question. "Mean. That kid is just plain mean."

"Finn?"

"Yes, mean as a wet wasp."

"He had big plans for Liam."

Cory's mom left the highway for the better side of town without responding. Cory thought of how Finn would brag about Liam's football skills and how Liam seemed to need his praise. He watched the world going by, cool grassy lawns beneath towering shade trees and homes with crisp white paint. Not a single broken or boarded window in sight. Up they climbed, higher and higher. Views of the city below appeared.

"Finn was going to manage his money," Cory explained, "and his uncle was going to open a nightclub down on Geddes Street. Liam always laughed, but I think he liked it."

"Awful." His mother clucked her tongue and shook her head. "Grown men making plans on the back of a little boy."

They turned off a main road and wound up a long street before his mother pulled over and tilted her head. "Is this it? Does it say 4444?"

"Yes, 'The Muillers,'" Cory said, pointing to a large tile worked into one of the columns that supported massive wrought iron gates. The gates stood open and his mom turned in, winding up a driveway bordered by trees, flower beds, and thick grass. The huge house was capped by a weather vane glinting with gold.

"Can you believe this?" Cory's words drifted from his lips.

"No," his mother said softly. "I can't."

They pulled into the circular driveway and parked behind a sleek blue Bentley sedan. Cory's mom wore a pale brown dress. Her purse matched its color, although its clasp was tarnished and broken so that he could see the box of breath mints inside. His own white shirt was stiff and uncomfortable, and when he looked at the reflection of their images in the side of the car, he removed his hand from hers. He did not want to look like a child. He was a football player. Football players were supposed to be big and tough.

His mother rang the bell. The sound of a large gong came from deep inside the house. The boy who answered the door was Cory's height. His blond hair was swept back from his forehead in a stylish cut. Instead of dressy clothes like Cory had on, he wore green gym shorts and a Boston Red Sox away-game T-shirt.

His teeth were perfect. "Hey, you must be Cory."

Cory smiled to hear his real name—not Flapjack.

"Hi, Mrs. Marco," said the boy. "I'm Jim. Everyone calls me Jimbo." He smiled. "Please come in. My parents and Coach McMahan are waiting to meet you."

Cory's mom gave Cory a "you better have good manners too" look, and they followed Cory's future teammate through a house with ceilings only a giant could reach. Fancy oil paintings covered the wood-paneled walls like medals on the chest of an army general. Even though he was excited, the smell of wood and leather and old books and the yellow light falling through the tall windows made Cory feel sleepy.

They passed a huge fireplace. There was a stuffed zebra's head above the mantle. Its eyes watched them all the way to the double glass doors, which were open to the warm evening breeze. On a granite terrace overlooking a gigantic pool, Coach McMahan stood next to Mr. Muiller. He was a large man, blond like his son, only with short hair and a close-cut beard. The men held bottles of high-end beer with necks wrapped in gold foil. They watched over a wide grill crowded with sizzling steaks and chops.

Jimbo's mother was blond too, and big. She sat at a long glass table, stirring ice in a tall glass. Behind her was a row of potted lemon trees and beyond them enormous hedges cut with the precision of Lego building blocks. Even farther off was a breathtaking view that stretched to Lake Ontario some fifty miles away. Posts surrounded the pool, each capped by an oil torch, their flames dancing in the breeze.

It was all like a dream to Cory, too much to take in.

"Hey, hey!" Coach McMahan raised his voice and his beer. "It's the Touchdown Kid!"

Cory felt his face warm. "Hi, Coach."

Mrs. Muiller jumped to her feet, and the grownups introduced themselves.

Cory shook hands with the grownups and said hello. Coach McMahan and Mr. and Mrs. Muiller all wore soft cotton polo shirts in bright colors, like the crayons that jump out at you from an open box. Even Mr. Muiller's pants were the color of a strawberry popsicle. Fat diamonds sparkled on Mrs. Muiller's fingers and wrists and from the bottoms of her ears. Cory glanced at his mom's purse and felt ashamed.

Mrs. Muiller turned to her son. "Jimbo, why don't you take Cory to the basement to see his room?"

"The *basement*?" Cory's mom scowled.

"Oh, not a basement like you're thinking," Mrs. Muiller said, pouring Cory's mom a drink from a beaded glass pitcher on the table.

"We have a walkout lower level with a rec room and bunk rooms for the kids and their friends, and then a wing for overnight guests. We love to entertain. Everyone is welcome here. It's busy all the time, especially during football season. Howard loves that grill, and the boys are always hungry."

"Come on." Jimbo nudged Cory in the ribs. He looked eager. "I'll show you."

Cory looked at his mom. She smiled uncomfortably but nodded for him to go. He followed Jimbo back into the house and down some carpeted stairs with thick wooden railings. Like everything else in the house, the rec room was enormous—practically a playground with flat-screen TVs; low, soft couches; beanbag chairs; Xbox machines; a pool table; and a Ping-Pong table as well. Along one wall stood half a dozen old-time arcade games, pinball and such. Cory stopped for a moment, amazed. Jimbo kept on walking down a wide, carpeted hall whose walls were lined with autographed jerseys of famous sports stars. Cory tried not to stare, but he couldn't help but notice that the collection included LeBron James, Peyton Manning, and Derek Jeter.

Halfway down the hall, Jimbo swung open a door and made a sweeping gesture. "Welcome to your new home."

Cory paused. He couldn't help thinking about the wire metal trap they used at home to keep the squirrels from nesting in their attic. They'd put peanut butter in there and the squirrels went for it every time.

Just a few steps in and *whap*, you had them.

16

The curtains were Vegas gold, patterned with the New Orleans Saints emblem. On the wall were life-size Fathead photos of Mark Ingram Jr. and Drew Brees. The lampshade, headboard, and bedspread all bore Saints emblems, and the rug was black. It was fantastic, if you were a crazed Saints fan, like Liam.

"Wow." Cory did his best to muster enthusiasm, even though he preferred the Atlanta Falcons. "Nice."

"That ball's signed by their Super Bowl team." Jimbo pointed to a glass case on the dresser.

"Nice."

Jimbo shrugged. "And, you got your own bathroom."

Since Jimbo turned the light on in there, Cory felt obligated to look, even though it sort of embarrassed him.

"Yuck!" Jimbo said at the smell. He lifted the cover off the toilet bowl. "Someone left you a present."

Cory looked—he couldn't help but look—and before he knew what was happening, he was bent over the sink, gagging.

Jimbo nearly doubled over with laughter before righting himself and saying, "Dude, whoever did that is disgusting. Must have been one of the guys yesterday."

Cory closed his eyes, but the disgusting pile that had been waiting for him wouldn't leave his mind, and now he actually smelled it. He gagged again. Part of Cory wanted to grab Jimbo by the neck and punch his face in. Another part of him felt like crying because it seemed to have ruined everything. The sparkle of getting a scholarship, being called the Touchdown Kid, and living with a rich host family was gone.

"Aw, don't look like such a wimp." Jimbo sniffed and dried his eyes on his sleeve. "You gotta have a sense of humor. You Westside guys are supposed to be tough. A little poop never hurt anyone. Even a big poop."

Cory forced a smile. "Yeah, you got me pretty good. I never saw a mess like that before."

"Hey, man, not me!" Jimbo glanced into the bowl with a quizzical look before flushing it. "This looks like the work of Mike Chester. Definitely gross, but —c'mon—you gotta admit it's pretty funny, like . . . welcome home. *Not.* But you're probably gonna see worse than that. HBS guys are a little crazy."

Cory's stomach rolled at the thought of seeing something like that again. He'd never heard of anything like it and wondered if all rich kids had this sort of sick humor.

"Come on, let's go eat." Jimbo chuckled. "If you can."

They passed through the game room to go out some glass

doors to the pool level. The smallest of the pool's three circles was a steaming hot tub. The middle looked like a shallow area with a volleyball net and a basketball hoop. The biggest part was a deeper shade of blue and had a diving board. Thickly padded lounge chairs circled the area in groups of two or four with low tables and umbrellas in between. Jimbo took it all for granted, leading Cory up an outside staircase that brought them to the terrace where the grown-ups were.

"Well," Jimbo said to everyone, "he loved it. Didn't you?"

"Uh, yes. It's amazing." Cory looked to see if his mom was having fun, but her smile seemed to be pasted on. "Really."

"Did you show him his own bathroom?" Jimbo's mom touched Cory's mom on the shoulder and leaned close, dropping her voice. "I think boys should have their own bathrooms, don't you?"

Cory's mouth fell open. He couldn't believe Mrs. Muiller was in on the toilet joke. That just couldn't be. Still, he studied her face for a secret sign of glee.

"I think if you can afford it, yes," Cory's mom said sweetly.

"Oh, of course," said Jimbo's mom, patting Cory's mom's arm. "I didn't mean anything by that, Ashley. Sometimes my mouth just gets out in front of me. No offense intended."

"None taken." Cory's mom sipped her drink and studied his face.

Cory looked away because he didn't want her tanking this whole thing just because he wasn't entirely comfortable. If he had to put up with some crude humor, that was a price worth paying along the road to the NFL. Jimbo was right about one thing: Cory needed to be tougher.

"Okay, everyone," Mr. Muiller said as he unloaded the grill and carried the huge platter of meat to the table. "Time to eat!" A heavy woman in a gray dress and white apron brought several other dishes out from the kitchen. After a toast to Cory, his mom, and HBS football, they began to eat. Cory worried that his mom would grow bored with all the football talk, but it wasn't to be helped. Even Mrs. Muiller had an opinion on the upcoming HBS season and Coach McMahan's new spread offense.

"Ground and pound and a vicious defense." Mrs. Muiller shook a half-eaten ear of corn. "That's how you won the last state championship for HBS."

Coach McMahan smiled gently. "The game is changing, Deb."

"Then why isn't Cory a receiver? If Jimbo is gonna be an all-state quarterback in a spread offense, why not a young Odell Beckham Jr.?" Mrs. Muiller turned to Cory's mother. "No offense intended."

"None taken," Cory's mom said automatically, but Cory could see she was annoyed.

Coach McMahan pointed a chewed-over rib bone at Cory. "When this young man doesn't run by people, he runs through them, or over them. You still need a potent runner in the spread, someone versatile."

His words relaxed Cory.

The woman who helped with the food—her name was Helga—brought out a tray of ice-cream sundaes in cone-shaped dishes. There were six in all, which puzzled Cory until he heard a voice shout from inside the house.

"I'm home!"

Jimbo put his face in one hand. "There goes the neighborhood."

Everyone looked, and what Cory saw made him forget about everything else.

Perfect wasn't the right word. Perfect was too lifeless. Perfect wasn't real, or interesting.

The girl marching toward the table in a crimson-and-silver soccer uniform was nearly as tall as the boys, but slender, like a willow branch. Her hair was a wild blond mane, thick and long, New Orleans Saints gold. She had round red cheeks and big blue eyes.

Mrs. Muiller introduced Cheyenne as Jimbo's older sister in a funny voice, and Cory wondered if she'd had too much to drink.

"Had them ten months apart," Mrs. Muiller said in a loud whisper, leaning close to Cory's mom. "You believe that?"

Cheyenne's deep blue eyes locked on Cory, and he forgot to breathe.

"Forsooth, the Touchdown Kid!" She passed by Cory,

lightly mussing his hair. "Forsooth, brother. Forsooth."

A chill scampered down the middle of Cory's back. She scooped up a sundae along with one of the long silver spoons and plopped down beside him as if they were old friends before crossing her bare, tan legs and digging in.

"She thinks she's Shakespeare." By the tone of Jimbo's voice and the way he pointed his long spoon, Cory could tell the two weren't friends. "She's obsessed."

"Methinks thou art but a knave." Cheyenne picked the cherry off the top of the sundae and dangled it over her mouth before dropping it in.

Cory now liked her as well as loved her.

"You think you're so smart?" Jimbo flashed a mean smile. "Then how come you're reading *Friends with Boys*?"

Cheyenne sighed and looked directly at her mother. "Deb, thy son needeth a lobotomy."

Cory tried to cover up his burst of laughter with a cough. Cory grinned at his mom but saw that she disapproved of Jimbo's sister.

Now Jimbo looked pointedly at Cory. "Maybe she's reading it because she's hot for Mike Chester, right? Maybe she's planning something."

Cory's mouth fell open because Cheyenne was blushing now and he had no idea how to react. He tried to take a bite from the sundae in front of him, but choked and spurted whipped cream onto his plate.

"It's enough to make you sick, right?" Jimbo smirked at Cory, nodding his head.

"No, that's okay," Cory sputtered in a lame attempt to come to Cheyenne's defense.

"Mike Chester happens to be an extremely *interesting* person." Cheyenne now glared at Cory, as if he were on the other side.

"He's a creeper," Jimbo sneered.

"*'A rose by any other name is still a rose.'*" She held her brother steady now in her gaze.

Suddenly, Mrs. Muiller hiccupped and burst into tears. "Oh, that poor boy, Coach McMahan. That poor Liam. He had a smile that could light up a room. Everyone said he was just perfect for the offense, and now he's got a ruined knee and he's stuck in that . . . that *place.*"

"Deb!" Mr. Muiller glared at his wife and angled his head toward Cory's mom.

Mrs. Muiller turned to Cory's mom. "Oh, I'm so sorry. I didn't mean anything by it. No offense. The Westside has some lovely homes, I'm sure. It's just that Liam was such a sweet boy with that sparkling smile. Do you know him at all?"

"We know Liam very well." Cory's mom squeezed her lips tight and used a napkin to wipe her mouth before turning to Coach McMahan. "Maybe this just wasn't meant to be."

She stood up. "Thank you for dinner. Come on, Cory. It's time to go."

"But, Mom—" Cory said, glancing back at Cheyenne.

"No buts, Cory." Cory's mom had him by the arm, and she moved him through the house fast, out the front door, down the steps, and into their car before the upset look on the faces of the Muiller family could fully register. Coach McMahan burst out the front door after them, yelling, "Please, wait," and hailing Cory's mom and blocking their escape until Cory's mom rolled down her window.

"What?" she asked.

Coach McMahan left his spot in front of the car and leaned down to her eye level. "Deb didn't mean anything."

"Right, 'no offense intended.'"

Coach McMahan forced a chuckle. "She feels bad for Liam. We all do. Football is an unforgiving game."

"Coach McMahan, I appreciate the opportunity you're

offering Cory, I really do, but that's too much." She angled her head toward the house and the people in it. "This whole thing is just too . . . much."

"I understand. But they're good people, really. And Cory would be very comfortable," Coach McMahan said. "I promise. But you think about it, will you? Don't say no right now. Sleep on it and we can talk tomorrow."

Coach McMahan waited until Cory's mom sighed and said, "All right, Coach. We can talk tomorrow, but I don't think it'll do any good."

"Okay, but we'll talk." Coach McMahan forced a smile and pointed at Cory. "I hope we get you, Cory. You'd have one heck of a career."

Coach McMahan straightened and thumped the roof of the car, as if sending them into battle. Cory's mom didn't say anything else, and they rode back to their neighborhood in silence. Cory kept thinking mostly about Cheyenne and wishing they could live under the same roof. It was during that thirty-minute car ride that Cory felt maybe he was changing. He didn't know if it was a good or a bad change, but it was surely a change.

He felt like he wasn't a momma's boy anymore, and he had to admit to himself that he'd been just that up until now. He'd never wanted to be anywhere that wasn't close to his mother. He'd needed the comfort of her presence, her strength, and her advice. Now, though, it seemed like he could get along okay without her. Now, it seemed like if he was near Cheyenne, that would do just fine.

He looked over at his mom as they pulled into the driveway

and felt a little guilty about his thoughts, but the guilt only made him that much more certain about what he wanted. It wasn't wrong to take Liam's place. Someone was going to, and he expected Liam would rather it be him than some kid from across town. He had his own dreams and he certainly wanted to chase them down. And, there was Cheyenne.

"What are you so starry-eyed about?" His mother had turned off the engine and was staring hard at him.

"What? Oh, nothing." He looked away at a car parked down the street from their house. It was even junkier than theirs, some rusted orange compact with one side caved in and a tiny red-rimmed spare tire for the rear wheel. He thought about saying he was thinking about that car and the accident it had been in, but stayed silent instead.

"Something," she said.

He blurted out the truth. "I want to play there, Mom. I want to go to HBS."

"That woman . . ." His mother flicked her hand. "Did you hear the girl call her 'Deb'? So disrespectful. And after that polite hello the boy didn't seem like anything to write home about either."

"I thought Cheyenne was nice." Cory looked through the windshield at their crumbing home.

"Men, you're all the same." His mom sounded like she'd swallowed rotten milk.

"What's that mean?" Cory looked at his mom and fought back a smile because he liked being thrown in with "men."

"A pretty blonde and you lose your senses."

Cory felt a blush in his cheeks and he shrugged. "I thought you liked smart people."

"Smart? She was a smart *aleck*; I don't know about smart."

"She quoted Shakespeare."

"How would you know?"

"It sounded like it. I saw something on the History Channel once."

"Fancy talk can't make up for manners," his mom said.

Cory knew when to quit, so he got out and headed for the front door, glad for the streetlight. He had just reached the steps when he heard a sharp whistle.

"Hey!" From the shadows between houses emerged two shapes, one short, the other tall and round. Cory knew his mom was right behind him, but still, the sudden appearance of the older boys loosened his insides so much that he had to pee.

"Hey, what?" Cory's mom was beside him now, completely unafraid as she faced off with Dirty and Hoagie, who were now on their porch.

"Hey, we don't like rats." Dirty scowled at Cory's mom and thrust his chin out at her.

"Yeah," Hoagie said, sounding as big and as dumb as he looked. "Rats."

"I'll give you a rat." Cory's mom shifted into a fighting stance, placing one foot forward and throwing back her shoulders. "Get off our property."

"Ain't your property," Dirty sneered. "You're renters, just like the rest of us, so don't you get high and mighty, rat momma. No one likes a rat who snitches to the police."

"I didn't." Cory shook his head.

"Oh yeah? Well, someone did, 'cuz I got picked up today and so did Finn, and everyone saw you in the cop car, squealing."

Cory was so flustered that he couldn't speak.

The *snick* sound of a knife blade opening sliced into the heavy silence between them.

The sharp metal edge glowed in the streetlight.

Without thinking, Cory stepped between the blade and his mom.

Slowly, Dirty raised the blade.

Everything else was frozen.

"Rats get cut, you know." Dirty's words were little more than a whisper.

Cory felt its point prick his cheek and he flinched, so he missed his mother's movement—cat quick—as she stepped around him and swung. She slapped Dirty's face so hard he dropped the knife. The sound seemed to echo like thunder.

Dirty staggered back, holding his face, black eyes glistening with tears left by the sudden impact.

A patrol car rounded the corner, heading down the street.

"Get out of here." Cory's mom snarled deep in her throat. "I *see* you again, or you *touch* my son, I'll pound you into taco meat.

"Go!" Cory's mom lunged, and both the boys melted into the darkness.

Moments later, the orange clunker fired up and took off with screeching tires. Cory made a mental note to keep watch for that car.

His mom snatched up the knife and closed the blade. "Are you okay?"

Cory nodded, but he felt like he'd been turned inside out. His mom took his arm and led him inside, where she turned on the lights to look at his cheek. "I thought he cut you, but there's no mark."

"I felt it," Cory said, running his trembling fingers over the spot, "but then you smacked him so quick. Mom, that was crazy."

"I didn't even think," she said. "I couldn't believe you stepped in front of me. Cory, don't do that."

Cory swelled with pride. "I had to."

"No." She shook her head. "No."

She hugged him hard, then let go and was all business about getting ready for bed because it was late and she had work in the morning. Cory was in bed wearing boxers and a T-shirt with the light on so he could read when his mom appeared with a sleeping bag and a pillow. She laid them out on the scrap of orange shag rug next to his bed. "I'll sleep better in here."

Cory was secretly glad for her company because he'd already imagined Dirty sneaking in through his window sometime during the night with a new knife clenched in his teeth like a pirate.

"But," she said, "you won't be able to read because I'll need

76

you to shut off the light so I can get to sleep."

Cory nodded and put his book down. His mom kissed his cheek and lay down on the floor. She turned on her side and sighed heavily. "I love you, Cory."

"I love you, too, Mom." He clicked off the light and lay back.

Soon, the sound of her light snoring lulled him to sleep.

When Cory's mom woke him the next morning, she was sitting on the edge of the bed and her voice was muffled. There was enough light from the street for him to make out her form, but not her face.

"What's wrong, Mom?" He sat straight up. "Why are you crying?"

Sobbing, she said, "Because we live in a place like this . . . and I'm sorry, Cory. I am so sorry that I didn't do better for you. Criminals with knives and boarded-up windows. You're all I *have* and I should've done better for you."

She groaned in pain.

Cory hugged her and held her tight. "Shh, don't say that, Mom. I love you. We're fine."

"No." She shook her head violently and her hair flew about her head like dark birds in the thin light. "No, we are *not* fine, but I'm not going to hold you back, Cory. I'm not."

"What . . . what do you mean?" he asked.

"This opportunity—at HBS. It's one you can't pass up, no matter how I feel. When Coach McMahan calls," she said, "I'm letting you go."

Cory stayed on at home for the final week of summer.

In the city, kids played youth-league football until high school, unlike in the suburbs and private schools, which fielded middle school teams whose seasons began with the start of school. When Coach McMahan spoke to Cory's mom and she accepted the HBS scholarship, he told her he preferred that Cory not practice and play with the Glenwood Cougars during his final week on the Westside.

"But he didn't say that I *couldn't*, right?" Cory asked after his mom had hung up the phone and told him what was said.

"No, he only said he preferred that you didn't because he didn't want you to get hurt."

That made Cory think of Liam, but freak accidents were like lightning—not apt to strike in the same place twice.

"I won't get hurt," he told his mom. "I want to play. It'll be my last game as a Cougar and I'll be the starter!"

Not only did Cory relish the thought of being treated like football royalty by his teammates and coaches—as he surely would with an HBS scholarship in hand—he simply loved being out on the gridiron. It was as he expected, too. At Tuesday night's practice, Cory got to line up with the first-team offense, kids deferred to him at the water hose, and it seemed like everyone enjoyed calling him by his new nickname. Coach Mellon, who suddenly treated Cory as well as he'd treated Liam, told the entire team—beaming with pride—that he'd personally heard Coach McMahan call Cory the Touchdown Kid on Sunday.

It was funny to Cory that Coach Mellon acted like they were old friends, and he took note of how quickly things changed now that he was a star on the field.

But he couldn't stop thinking about Liam. Liam remained in the hospital and, despite the way Finn had treated them the first time, Cory's mom agreed that they should visit his best friend now that he'd recovered from surgery a bit more. On Thursday, his mom got off work a little early and they headed to the hospital.

Cory was relieved to see only Liam's mom by his bedside. She looked tired and sad, like some haggard storybook witch who'd lost her powers. Her dress was gray and wrinkled, and bluish-green veins stood out on her pale, thin legs.

Liam had the TV on above his bed. His leg still hung in the air, and the cast was open at the knee, exposing a horror show of red and purple flesh. A tube sucked yellow fluid from the wound into a machine that pumped vigorously from its own stand at the far side of the bed.

When he saw Cory walk into the room, Liam's face lit up and he snapped the TV off. "Cory! Thanks for coming. Wait, can I call you Cory?"

"Why wouldn't you?"

"Coach Mellon came by." Liam grinned. "He said something about the 'Touchdown Kid'?"

Cory laughed. "Oh, that. Well, I had a good day Sunday."

"Yeah, after they turned my leg into dog food, right?"

Cory glanced at Liam's mom. She stared at the floor and her lips moved without sound. Then he looked at his own mom for help.

"It won't keep *you* down, Liam," Cory's mom said.

"No, ma'am," Liam said. "I'll be back, and then my buddy's gonna be my backup again."

They all laughed.

"Give me a little time to enjoy it, will ya?" Cory said.

Liam's face got suddenly serious and he nodded at the open wound. "They said a year and a half . . ."

Then he brightened again. "But you know me, I'll heal faster than that and I'll have two seasons with the Cougars A team to knock Coach McMahan's socks off, get that scholarship, and rain all over your parade, my friend, so you keep my seat warm, will ya?"

"I'll be a little busy, Touchdown Kid and all," Cory said. "But I will make sure someone keeps a seat nice and warm for you on the bench."

"Hey, you're lucky they got me tied down here." Liam raised his arm, which was attached to an IV line.

"I am lucky," he said in a whisper. Suddenly, Cory felt incredibly sad. Tears welled up in his eyes and he choked back a sob.

The room got quiet except for the whir of the pump.

"Oh, we brought you something." Cory's mom produced a hefty bag of candy corn from her purse.

"Hey, my favorite." Liam took the bag and opened it, popping a few in his mouth before offering some to his mom. "They brought my favorite, Ma."

His mother just shook her head and sniffed. "Finn'll be here soon."

Cory and Liam stared at each other until Cory softly said, "I didn't tell."

"I know." Liam laid his head back and sighed. "Finn knows too. They let him go."

"They can't prove nothin'." Liam's mom looked up with an unexpected burst of fire in her eyes.

"Well," Cory's mom said, "we better let you rest."

Liam nodded and closed his eyes for a moment. "Yeah. I get tired with these painkillers, but thanks for coming by. And Cory?"

"Yeah?"

Liam looked at him with moist eyes. "I'm glad it's you taking my place . . ."

"Yeah? Really?"

Liam nodded.

"Thanks, Liam." Cory and his mom turned to go.

"Cory?"

Cory stopped and looked back. "Yeah?"

Liam had his eyes closed and he yawned. "Tell Cheyenne I said hi, will you?"

"Sure, Liam."

"Tell her I'm still gonna wear crimson and silver. It's just gonna take me a little longer."

Cory and his mom stayed quiet as they rode the elevator and left the hospital. When they reached her car, his mom sighed. "That poor, poor boy."

"Why, Mom?" Cory said. "He'll be back."

Cory's mom hesitated, staring at him across the roof of her battered car. "Cory, your friend will be lucky if he can even walk."

Cory swallowed.

"I hate this sport," she said. "I hate it and I'm asking myself why I'd even allow it."

Cory felt a chill.

"I'm serious, Cory," she said. "I know what I said about opportunity, but . . . something is telling me to pull the plug on this whole thing."

Cory's mom was upset and silent during the car ride home, but she got over her concerns by the time they reached their house.

After practice on Saturday morning, Cory's mom took him shopping. It seemed like she spent a lot of her savings on clothes she called "decent enough" for him to wear at a private school that required collars and didn't allow shorts or jeans. They bought two pairs of khaki pants and five Walmart-brand collared shirts from the sale rack. A brown pair of boat shoes from the thrift store finished the look.

"This'll get you started," she said. "Coach McMahan said you can't go to school without a collared shirt."

As a going-away present of sorts, Cory's mom splurged for them to see the new Marvel superhero movie at the mall. Cory had been to very few movies at the theater, and he loved the high-backed stadium seats. It made him nervous when an usher went by because he and his mom had stashed candy and two cans of soda inside her purse.

When the usher was out of sight, Cory's mom leaned over and whispered, "Don't worry. He doesn't care. I bet he wouldn't pay seven dollars for a box of Milk Duds either."

The movie was grand, and after dinner, Cory's mom slept on his floor again because she said she'd miss him.

"I won't be far," he told her.

The next morning, they woke to a downpour. The Cougars game was away at a field north of the city in Central Square. A wooded hill flooded the field that already looked worn-out. Puddles of mud scattered across the soupy grass promised a sloppy day. As Cory chugged through the mud, gripping the ball tight in both hands, slipping after another two-yard gain, he began to wish he'd listened to Coach McMahan's advice and stayed home.

Football in a wet, muddy mess was fun so long as you didn't have your sights set on dazzling people with your brilliant running ability. Cory was able to score the game's only touchdown on an eleven-yard off-tackle play, but that was it. The game ended with Glenwood winning 6–0 and the entire team brown with mud and wet to the bone.

The good-bye with his teammates and coaches was a hurried affair in the downpour. No one really seemed to care, even Cory. His mom covered the passenger seat with two old bath towels. Even though the temperature was in the mid-sixties, Cory shivered and turned on the heat. He couldn't wait to get home.

"HBS doesn't play on sloppy fields like that," Cory said as

they zipped down the highway. "You can bet on that."

"Hmm." Cory's mom seemed to have her mind on something else as she peered between slaps of the windshield wipers.

At home, Cory wiggled and wriggled out of his sopping uniform and equipment. He'd never thought about a shower as a wonderful thing before, but that's how it felt as he stepped out, clean and warm.

"Well, no picnic today." Cory's mom pointed at the kitchen window. She had prepared a picnic lunch with the plan being for the two of them to head out to Green Lakes State Park.

They ate at the kitchen table instead and watched old DVDs all afternoon. Cory was exhausted from the game and nerves. Tomorrow was Labor Day.

It was his last night on Hope Avenue.

The rain continued on through the night, and Cory woke the next morning to more gray skies.

His mom was already up, and her sleeping bag lay on his floor, an empty nest. He smelled French toast on his way down the stairs.

"I heard you in the bathroom so I started cooking." His mom wore a thin, worn-out purple robe, and she raised her spatula for him to see. "I know it's your favorite."

After they ate, his mom removed a TracFone from her purse and handed it to him.

"Mom." His tone scolded her for spending money on him. "You already spent too much on all those clothes . . . and the movie."

"It wasn't much, and there's only ninety minutes on it," she said. "But if you need me, you use it. I don't care when or where, Cory. I'm not abandoning you. I can always come and get you."

"Who said you're abandoning me?" He squeezed the small phone and thought about the HBS football program, those crimson and silver colors, the players like knights from a storybook. "I need to go, Mom. I want this. It's my chance, an opportunity."

"I know. I'll just . . . I'm going to miss you is all."

The rain never let up, and they spent their last day together shut in, watching more DVDs from the library, some old favorites. It was like his mom had known they'd be alone together stuck in the house, even though the weatherman hadn't forecasted the rain.

Each movie seemed to bring them back to a specific time in their lives, each one special. There was *Rudy* from when Cory first started playing football at age nine. *Babe* reminded them both of when he started school, and *The Lion King* was when they'd talked about how his dad was never coming back. Neither of them talked about how the movies made them feel, but Cory knew they shared the exact same memories.

Finally, Coach McMahan's big white SUV pulled into the driveway at 6:30 p.m. just as the rain stopped. School at HBS began the next morning, and with it, practice for the sixth-grade football team. The coach took Cory's lone, battered suitcase and put it in the back before shaking hands with Cory's mom, assuring her he'd be fine, and climbing back into the truck.

Cory turned to his mom.

"The head coach himself coming for you," she said, tweaking his ear. "You must be pretty special, I'd say."

"I'll see you Saturday after practice?"

"Sure will," she said, "and I'll get another good movie for Saturday night, even if I have to pay for one. We could even go to the theater."

"You don't have to do that, Mom."

She bit her lip and her eyes filled up to their brims. "I'll be saving a lot of money on groceries. Those Muillers have no idea what they're in for."

She forced a laugh and then looked past him at the coach. "You better go. He's waiting. You got your phone?"

"Yes." Cory hugged her.

After a moment, she pushed him away and sniffed, her face twisted with pain. "You go."

Cory turned and went. He climbed into the passenger side and waved to her as they backed out of the narrow driveway. As they pulled away, she stopped waving, covered her mouth, and turned toward the broken house.

"Yeah," Coach McMahan said, turning the corner, "it's always tough that first time, but it has to happen, and you're getting a heck of an opportunity, Cory."

The sun was setting, but it was suddenly naked and bright and it glinted off the wet road, causing Coach McMahan to put on sunglasses.

"I know." Cory tried to sound excited, but he just couldn't. It was all he could do to keep from flinging open the door and jumping out at the next stop sign and running back home. He felt ashamed that he'd thought being around Cheyenne could make him forget his mom.

"Yeah, always a little glum." The coach shucked a piece of

Wrigley's Spearmint gum and offered one to Cory. "That's why now I come ready to these pickups. I got a surprise." The coach glanced at him. "Wanna bet it cheers you up?"

"Okay," Cory said. "Sure."

"Okay. I bet you ten push-ups." Coach McMahan pulled up to a red light and reached behind Cory's seat. "Take a look at *this*."

At first Cory thought it was a blanket, then some kind of flag, before Coach McMahan shook it out, and then he could see it was a crimson-and-silver HBS football jersey, glimmering in the late-day light.

"Take it," the coach said, "it's yours. Look at the name. You like 28?"

"I . . ." Cory was speechless. "How did you know?"

"Adrian Peterson, right?" Coach McMahan nodded his head as the light turned green and he began to drive again. "I asked your mom who your favorite player was. I'd have hesitated giving you a number like that if I hadn't seen you run with my own eyes."

The crimson and silver made it kind of *look* like an Adrian Peterson jersey from when he was at Oklahoma, only stitched onto the back was: MARCO.

Cory felt flushed. "This is what the sixth-grade team wears?"

"That's the game jersey, yeah. Nice, huh? Try it on."

"Super nice." Cory pulled the jersey over his head. It slipped on, silky soft and smelling all new. He tugged it out in front of him and looked down at the number, beaming with pride.

"We like to do things right at HBS, Cory. I really think you'll love it."

Coach McMahan drove for a few minutes before he spoke again. "Look, you're not going to see me much after this. I'm busy with the varsity, but bringing in our scholarship guys is a big deal. We only have two scholarship sixth-graders and then two ninth-graders. It's an honor. You know that a lot of time and money will be invested in you, so it's important that everything you do reflects well on the program. You understand?"

"Yes." Cory was so full of good intentions he felt like he'd burst. "Thank you, Coach. I won't let you down. I swear on my life."

When they arrived at the Muillers' gigantic house, Cory was surprised to see the driveway crowded with cars pulled off to the side.

"What's going on?" he asked.

"I told you this is a big deal," Coach McMahan said. "The Muillers are throwing a welcome party for you. It's kind of an HBS tradition."

"Wow, I wish my mom could have been here." The words escaped Cory before he could consider if they were rude or not.

"It's really a guys-only thing, and this is your new family, Cory. Your mom will always be there for you—she's your mom—but these people will have your back, day in and day out. It's like a bunch of brothers and uncles and cousins. Now, you won't like them all the same, but they'll stick by you for the next seven years. That's one of the great things about being an HBS player. So, get your suitcase and head right in."

"You're . . . not coming?" Cory felt a bit let down.

Coach McMahan looked at his watch. "I got a coaches' meeting, game film to break down. We play FM on Friday night. I just wanted to deliver you here and start you off right. Go ahead. You'll be fine."

Coach McMahan made a shooing motion with his hand. "The Muillers will take great care of you. They want you here. Jimbo's got some potential, but it's a lot easier for college scouts to spot a kid if he's on a championship team. The Muillers know you don't win titles in high school football without a dominant runner."

"And . . . that's me?"

"That's what we're all banking on." Coach McMahan stroked his concrete chin. "You'll have to work hard, but . . . what I saw from you in that game when you took over for Liam? I've never seen anything like it before, and I wouldn't be surprised if I never see it again. And that's saying something, because I watch a *lot* of football. I mean, I've been calling you Touchdown Kid kind of for a laugh, but it's not a joke. You've got a nose for the end zone."

Cory felt dizzy with pride. Only a little more than a week ago, he had a coach calling him Flapjack and saying he'd never be a real football player. Now this. People were counting on him, banking on him. The Touchdown Kid.

"Thanks, Coach."

"You're very welcome, Cory. Now get in there. It's time to begin a new chapter in your life. Maybe the best you'll ever have."

Cory shook hands with the coach and got his suitcase out of the back. He stopped at the front door to turn and wave to Coach McMahan, but all he saw were the taillights to the big white SUV disappearing around the last bend in the driveway.

Cory rang the bell and Mr. Muiller answered the door with a big smile. "Hi, Cory. Welcome. You ready for this?"

Mr. Muiller had Cory put his suitcase beneath the watchful zebra mounted on the wall and then headed straight out onto the terrace. There wasn't another person in sight. The trees dripped and hissed in the breeze. The tremendous view looked drab beneath the hurrying clouds. The granite terrace was still damp from rain, and the umbrellas were soggy. The only sign of life was the slowly smoking grill. It didn't make sense. He'd seen all the cars, but the place was deserted.

Mr. Muiller marched right up to steps leading down to the pool and stopped. When Cory caught up to him, the evening exploded with a shout:

"Welcome to the HBS Football Family!"

The words were followed by a storm of cheering and applause, all for him.

Nearly seventy people—fathers and their sons—were

crammed around the edges of the pool. The players wore their jerseys—like Cory—and the dads had on crimson-and-silver golf shirts and shorts; some even wore HBS crimson hats. Cory had to catch his breath. He looked up at Mr. Muiller, who grinned down at him. "Welcome, Cory. Or should I say Touchdown Kid?"

Cory smiled wide. "Thanks."

Then Mr. Muiller shouted, "Okay, boys, let's get these steaks on the grill!"

There was another cheer and people began to file up the wide staircase from below. Each person made it his business to welcome Cory personally.

"Great to have you, Cory."

"Welcome! You're gonna love it!"

"We're so glad you're one of us."

"Welcome to HBS."

"Glad the weather cleared up for you."

"Hey, Touchdown Kid!"

"Congratulations."

Cory grinned and thanked everyone, shaking all the fathers' hands. He was so happy, but he still wished his mom could have been there, not only to see how he was being treated, but so she could share his joy. It was a guys' thing though, and it was hard not to have fun.

Someone handed him a Sprite and someone else offered him pretzels from a bowl. The smell and sound of sizzling steaks filled the air. When Cory turned his head away from the flaming steaks, a six-foot monster of a kid with a big wooly afro and an outstretched hand had appeared in front of him.

"What's up, bro? I'm Dana Gant. Everybody just calls me Gant."

"Hey." Cory was awed by Gant's size and amazed that he was only in sixth grade.

"Guess you and me are the only ones without a dad here tonight," Gant said. "Check this out, Mexican jumping beans."

Gant unfolded his meaty hand and, indeed, three small beans twitched in his palm.

"Kinda neat," Cory said.

"Yeah, I won them at the fair." Gant smiled down on his beans.

"Is your dad away for work or something?" Cory asked.

"No." Gant snapped his hand shut and clenched his jaw. "No idea where the man is."

"Oh. Yeah." Cory felt dumb for asking and his mind spun, searching for a good way out. "My dad died, so I guess I could say the same."

"Naw, you could say 'heaven' if you wanted to, and people would feel bad for you. Me? He's just *gone*." Sleepy lids hid half of Gant's big brown eyes, but his smile was bright and full of energy.

"I mean, I guess you got Mr. Muiller and I got Mr. Trimble, but, you know . . ." Gant emptied the beans into his pocket and shrugged. "Either way, we're both scholarship kids, so we gotta stick together. I heard you're from the Westside."

"Right," Cory said. "You?"

Gant gave his head a shake. "The Pool. Liverpool. No way like here, where we come from."

"No way for sure," Cory said, returning Gant's smile.

"I been here for a year already. Trimbles live a couple streets away. Big house—not as big as this, but big. First fifth-grader they ever gave a scholarship to."

"Coach McMahan told me about you," Cory said.

"Yeah, played on the youth team last year and went to HB Elementary to get ready. Lots of the kids here go to HB Elementary, but not all."

"Oh."

"Next thing they'll do is recruit a couple wide receivers for ninth grade," Gant said. "Then Jimbo's gonna have everything he needs."

"What do you mean?"

Gant shrugged. "They got me to protect his blindside. You give us a run game to keep teams from blitzing all day. Once he has some receivers, your new brother Jimbo is gonna be ready for all-state."

Cory was surprised that the HBS people had things planned out so well, but all he had to do was look around to realize they meant business.

"Well, steak time." Gant lowered his voice. "And there's no limit. They just keep feeding you here. These people are *rich*."

Gant patted his big belly and headed for the grill, where people had begun lining up with plates. Gant looked back at him and motioned to come on, but the excitement and the Sprite left Cory wanting a bathroom. He remembered seeing one near the zebra room. Signaling that he'd be back to Gant, he let himself back into the house. The big glass door muted the noise of the party, and Cory heard his own loud breathing as he marched across the room.

He used the bathroom and washed his hands.

When Cory switched off the light and opened the door, someone grabbed a fistful of his new jersey and shoved him backward into the dark bathroom, slamming him into the wall.

"What are you *doing*?" Cory wished he sounded tougher than he did.

Whoever held him switched on the light.

Cory stood face-to-face with a boy he hadn't noticed outside, a tough-looking kid with a jet-black crew cut and a thin, bleached scar on his upper lip. His pasty white skin burned with red blotches of fury.

"You think you get to just waltz right in here and be the star?" the kid snarled. "Touchdown Kid—please. *I'm* the running back for HBS, this year and every year to come. They picked you out of the gutter and you're supposed to be some tough guy from the Westside? Well, I don't give a crap where you're from, you're not tougher than *me. Mike Chester.*"

"I . . . I never said I was." Cory swallowed and pushed at

the boy's hand, but his grip only tightened and he pressed Cory harder into the wall.

"That's right, you're not." The boy licked his lips. "And I don't care what anyone says, coaches, players, parents . . . I know, and now *you* know, that's my spot. If they try to give it to you, I don't care. I'll take it back. It's mine."

The boy moved his face even closer to Cory's, so that their noses almost touched. "And you don't even *look* at Cheyenne. You got that?"

"I didn't," Cory squeaked.

"And *don't*. Not even from the corner of your eye."

After one final shove, the boy turned and shut off the light, slammed the door, and left Cory standing there in the dark feeling foolish.

26

Cory's hands shook as he reached for the door handle to let himself back out onto the deck and into the gut of the party. People were talking and laughing and sitting or standing around cocktail tables, plates heavy with big, thick steaks they cut with sharp, wood-handled knives and then chewed with open mouths. Cory glanced here and there for a sign of Chester, remembering the taunts between Jimbo and Cheyenne about him. Cory wondered—and it would make sense, he thought— if Chester had simply waited for his chance to get Cory alone and wasn't staying for the rest of the welcome party.

He found Jimbo with a couple players whose names he didn't remember and fell into their conversation, nodding and laughing on cue.

Jimbo turned to him. "Hey, get some food, superstar."

Cory studied Jimbo's face for signs of a conspiracy with

Chester, but saw none. It had sounded like Jimbo didn't have any fondness for Mike, and now Cory knew why. What kind of teammate would ambush Cory—the guest of honor—in the bathroom? A creeper, wasn't that what Jimbo had called him?

The mystery was Cheyenne. Could she really be connected to someone so awful? It didn't seem possible. That would devastate him.

"I'm no superstar." Cory spoke softly and cast his eyes at the floor.

"Aw." Jimbo slugged his shoulder. "You gotta get used to that. We are going to rule the league, sixth grade, seventh, eighth, freshman, and varsity. State title. That's what this whole thing is about, and you're gonna be a huge part of it. Every defense in the game knows they gotta stop the run. When they load up to slow you down, the passing game is gonna open up for me like a set of double doors at a Christmas sale."

"I'm sure you guys have more than one person to run the ball." Cory watched Jimbo carefully.

Jimbo looked annoyed. "Don't tell me. Did Mike Chester just give you an earful?"

"Uh, you could say that."

"He's an idiot." Jimbo looked around for Mike. "Don't listen to him. He's in love with himself, but no one else is."

"Not Cheyenne?"

Jimbo studied Cory's face. "Oh, don't you fall for that, too."

"Fall for what?" That's what he said, but he knew just what Jimbo meant. He could see her big blue eyes and that pretty smile framed by golden hair without even closing his eyes.

"My sister. She smiles and people get goofy, but she's not what you think and you'll just make a fool out of yourself."

Cory felt himself blushing because even though he wanted to protest, he couldn't deny he'd already fallen for Cheyenne. To hide his feelings, he loaded a plate with food and sat down at the big table. Suddenly he remembered sitting and eating there with his mother over a week ago.

"Can I sit here?"

Cory looked up at a husky kid with big white teeth and tight curly blond hair. "Sure."

"Parker Leikam," the boy said, taking a seat. "I'm Jimbo's backup. You like the Patriots?"

"I'm a Falcons fan."

"Falcons?" Parker scrunched up his face. "NFC South? Well, as long as you're not a Ravens fan . . ."

"What's wrong with the Ravens?" A thick, neckless boy introduced himself as Garrison Green and sat down as well.

"What's *right* with them?" Parker asked.

Gant appeared and sat as well. "Don't get these two going on that junk. They're best friends, but they'll argue all night if you let 'em."

"You play middle linebacker or something?" Cory asked Garrison, cutting into his steak.

Garrison grinned. "You got it. Fullback, too. I know we're gonna run mostly spread, but when you get into the red zone? You gotta run the ball there, and *I'm* the guy who's gonna lead you to pay dirt."

"He doesn't need a fullback," Gant scoffed. "Coach McMahan says this here's the Touchdown Kid. You think he needs you? You should be joining me on the line. That's the spot."

"Line? I'm too athletic for the line," Garrison said. "You ever see me dance?"

"Yeah," Parker said. "I know you like to dance, but you gotta stop dressing up in that pink tutu."

They all laughed.

The four of them ate and then sat talking football until darkness overran the sky and people began to bleed away. Jimbo appeared and gripped Cory's shoulders. "You guys making my main man feel at home?"

"He's the secret to your success," Garrison said, "so you better keep rubbing his shoulders."

"That I won't do, but I'll grace you mopes with my presence." Jimbo sat down and cracked a soda, and they had a discussion about what position was the most important to a football team. Each of them argued for his own position and it made for some good laughs.

Cory warmed to his newfound friends. He sensed that they respected and liked him already, and he felt he could trust them. He waited for a pause in the chatter before he asked, "Hey, what do you guys think about this Mike Chester kid?"

Garrison narrowed his eyes. "He put raccoon poop in my sleeping bag on our Cub Scout overnight. He said it wasn't him, but I know it was."

"He does seem to like poop," Cory said, giving Jimbo a knowing look to remind him of the toilet last week.

Garrison nodded and continued, "Back in fourth grade, he beat up Parker when he wouldn't share his Skittles."

Cory raised his eyebrows, because even though Parker was a quarterback, he was no wilting flower. His legs were thick as tree trunks.

Parker nodded his head, then blushed and studied the table-top. "I shared, but not the red ones. He's got a black belt, you know, and he's pretty crazy."

"Bet you got all kinds of crazies on the Westside though, right Cory?" Jimbo looked and sounded eager, like he meant no offense.

A quick replay of *real* crazies flashed through Cory's mind: the kid who cut his own sister with a razor, the kid who lit fire to the back seat of his grandfather's car, the kid who hung people's cats from their porch railings. He was pretty sure fights over Skittles were as common as cockroaches, but all he said was, "Nah, not really."

After the last guest had departed, and Helga was busy cleaning up, Mr. Muiller produced two sports mouthpieces and helped Cory and Jimbo mold them for the next day.

"We start right out hitting at HBS," Mr. Muiller said. "Because we're a private school, we can do things our own way, and these guys have been doing drills all summer. You should be fine. You've been practicing for weeks now, right?"

Cory nodded. He took the U-shaped rubber piece Mr. Muiller removed from a boiling saucepan and chomped down on it so it molded to his teeth. Peppermint flooded his mouth.

"Wow. Tastes good," Cory said, speaking around the rubber guard, amazed at how good rich kids had it.

"Keep your teeth closed," Mr. Muiller said.

When they had finished, Mr. Muiller ushered them into

the zebra room, where he covered up a yawn and asked Cory if he needed anything.

"I think I'm set." Cory held up the peppermint mouthpiece, then hoisted his suitcase off the floor.

"Oh, let me show you something." Mr. Muiller put a finger in the air and motioned with it for Cory to follow him down the hall and into the grand entryway. Jimbo followed along too. On the wall beside the front door was a glowing touch pad.

"Alarm system. You'll need the code." Mr. Muiller tapped out four numbers. "Four fours, simple, then press the Arm button to set it before you leave. Four fours again and Disarm to shut it off. You'll have thirty seconds if you come in the house to disarm it, plenty of time. You'll hear it beeping, so don't worry about forgetting it, and you really won't have to arm it. We'll take care of that."

Mr. Muiller yawned again and smiled sleepily. "Got it?"

"Sure." Cory stared at the red light telling him the system was armed. "Four fours."

"Then Disarm," Jimbo said.

"Yes," Cory said.

"Four, like a lucky four-leaf clover," Jimbo said. "It's also the street number of our house."

"I got it." Cory tried not to sound impatient, but he wanted to be alone.

"Great. Well, you know where your room is. Make yourself at home." Mr. Muiller turned to his son. "Jimbo, you get to bed too. Big day tomorrow. Middle school. Big, big day."

Jimbo followed his dad up the stairs, turning to give Cory a wink. "See ya."

Cory took a deep breath and wound his way through the house, down the stairs, and into his bedroom. He set down his suitcase and headed straight for the bathroom, wanting to get it over with.

The toilet lid was up. He reached for the handle, trying not to see or smell, but realized that the bowl was empty.

"Oh." The sound of his own voice in the empty bathroom made him chuckle and shake his head.

He went back out into the bedroom to unpack his things and cried out when he saw Cheyenne sitting on the big chair in the corner.

"Did I scare you?" Cheyenne crossed one of her long, tan legs over the other. White shorts crept toward her waist and a turquoise T-shirt set her eyes ablaze. Her blond hair was pulled back into a ponytail, exposing the length of her neck.

Cory lost his breath.

"Cat got your tongue?" Her teeth sparkled.

"What's that mean?" He narrowed his eyes, suspicious.

Her laughter danced on little puffs of air. "Just that you were speechless—but now you're not. *'Be checked for silence, but never taxed for speech.'*"

Warnings from both Mike Chester and Jimbo swam through his mind briefly before sinking to the bottom of his brain. "What are you doing here?"

Her smile crept higher yet. Slowly, with a single crimson fingernail, she traced the line of her earlobe. "Welcoming you."

She might as well have punched his stomach full force.

"Do you know why?" she asked in a soft, scratchy voice.

Cory shook his head.

"You're cute, that's why. And I like you. You're nice."

His heart pounded inside his ribs, desperate to be free. He needed to think. She just sat there, grinning at him. Cory had no idea what to do. The thought of kissing her came and went, ushered out the door by complete terror.

Then, she stood up and spoke in a normal voice. "Don't act so excited."

"What do you mean?" He wondered if he had insulted her somehow.

"I mean, act like you don't care about any of this." She spoke in a friendly way and waved her hands around, suggesting the entire house. "Act like you don't care about state championships or the number 28. Don't be so eager to please everyone. That's how you'll get along. Liam had that, not a care in the world. He'd have done really well at HBS. You, I'm not so sure of. You care too much."

She stepped closer to him and touched the end of his nose, speaking softly again. "But I'm here to help. That's what big sisters are for . . ."

She briefly puckered her lips, kissing the air between them, and dropped one last little jangle of laughter before disappearing through the door.

Cory's nose tingled long into the night.

Her words circled his thoughts as he asked himself what she was really up to. Two things he knew: a poor night's sleep and acting like he didn't care to his new football coaches would not help him win the starting job at running back. Was that her game? Getting him sidetracked so Mike Chester would outshine him? Could she be that devious?

Cory picked the TracFone his mother had given him up off the night table. He turned it on and dialed his mother's number, pausing his thumb above the Send button. She'd said any time, any place, and that he wasn't alone. Then why did he feel so totally alone? So completely abandoned?

He set the phone down and rolled over. HBS was where he needed to be. Dreams didn't just grow on trees. They had to be forged from sweat and blood and sacrifice.

Maybe he was making a big deal out of nothing.

Maybe tomorrow, after a good night's sleep, it would all make sense.

Maybe it would all be good.

28

Cory was lying next to Liam in his hospital bed, also with his leg strung up to the ceiling and casted in white plaster from hip to toe. They were talking without words, and Cory knew Liam was upset with him. "It's not my fault. I had to take it. You couldn't, and like you said to me, maybe in ninth grade we'll be together." All this he willed Liam to understand until a slick, slithery snake on the pillow began to wiggle its way into Cory's ear.

In terror, Cory jumped up from the bed, torn from sleep and the very weird dream.

Jimbo was laughing and wiggling a slobbery wet finger at Cory. "Hahaha. Wake up, sleepyhead! Wet willy wakeup!"

"Oh . . . aw . . . oh . . ." Jimbo caught his breath. "You came out of that bed like your pants were on fire. Hahaha."

"Funny." Cory swiped the sheet from the bed and rammed

it into his ear, worming it in deep to soak up Jimbo's spit.

"Liam would've loved that." Jimbo sniffed and sighed. "'Course, Liam probably wouldn't have overslept."

"I'm not Liam." Cory stormed into the bathroom and slammed the door.

Jimbo called, "I'm telling you, you gotta be able to take a joke. They'll make mincemeat out of you in the locker room if you can't take a joke. C'mon, breakfast is ready, and the train leaves in twenty minutes."

Cory brushed his teeth and got ready. He threw on some new tan khaki pants with a collared navy shirt and his boat shoes. He slipped the tiny TracFone into his pants before hurrying upstairs. Helga was busy in the kitchen. Mr. Muiller was gone, his empty place marked by a crust of toast and smears of yellow yoke on a plate at the head of the table. Mrs. Muiller peered out at the world over a steaming mug of coffee she held in both hands. Jimbo and Cheyenne were just finishing.

"Breakfast is at seven sharp, Cory." Mrs. Muiller wore a fresh dose of makeup, but she sounded as tired as she looked. "There's an alarm clock right next to the bed. Not sure how they do things in your neck of the woods, but around here, you need to get a good breakfast."

"Sorry, ma'am." Cory set his backpack beside the chair with a plate of toast and eggs in front of it and took his place opposite Jimbo.

"No sorrys needed," Mrs. Muiller chirped pleasantly. "We aren't big with sorrys here, are we, kids? Life's too doggone short."

Cory stayed focused on his food, inhaling it as quickly as he

112

could and wondering if the Muillers had some kind of family rule about eating in silence.

"Seven twenty," Mrs. Muiller sang. She set her coffee mug down and both her kids scrambled up from their places. They slung backpacks over their shoulders and marched toward the garage with Cory in tow. Cory sat in back of the black Range Rover with Cheyenne, the seat between them seeming as big as a continent.

The day was bright and warm, but Cory felt like an alien from another planet as they drove twenty minutes and pulled up to the gray stone school. The two enormous wings on either side of the main entrance reminded Cory of some old prison out of a movie.

"You just go with Jimbo," Mrs. Muiller said, hurrying him to get out because her Range Rover was holding up a long line of cars and SUVs. "You'll get your schedule in homeroom and figure things out. Sink or swim, right? No offense. Now shut that door."

Cory nodded and shut the door, grateful to see Jimbo waiting for him, even if he wore a frown. Cheyenne was already jogging up the stone steps, plaid skirt skipping up off her bare legs. Cory fell in alongside Jimbo and remembered to try and look like he didn't care.

The next couple of hours were a whirlwind for Cory. His first three classes were with Jimbo, and then he had science with Gant.

He grabbed a seat next to his new friend and tried to get his bearings.

"Hey, Cory. How's it going so far?"

"Uh, okay, I guess. There's a lot going on."

"Oh, sure," Gant replied as he jammed his fist into his pocket. "See?" Gant opened his palm and two beans jiggled there.

"What happened to the other one?" Cory asked.

Gant furrowed his brow. "It quit on me, so I left it home to rest up."

"Did you ever think about letting them out?" Cory asked.

"What? Who?"

"Whatever it is that's inside those things."

Gant poked one of them. "No idea how I'd do that. They're just beans."

"Something's inside them or they wouldn't jump like that," Cory said. "That's all I'm saying. It's trapped."

The teacher began her lesson, so they got quiet. After science, the two of them went to lunch, and Cory realized he didn't have a lunch and he didn't have any money. In all the excitement he'd forgotten to ask.

"Uh, hey, Gant." Cory nudged him.

"Yeah?"

"Can I borrow a dollar or two? I'll pay you back."

Gant scowled. "What for?"

"Lunch."

"Lunch? You don't need money for lunch." Gant's face relaxed. He took a tray and handed one to Cory. "We're scholarship kids. We eat for free. It's part of the package."

"Really? How do they know who's who?" Cory asked.

"Look around." Gant lowered his voice.

"Yeah, so?" Cory just saw a bunch of kids.

"See their shirts with the little alligators on them, or the polo horses?"

"I guess so."

"Yeah, our shirts don't have that." Gant tugged at his very large, red collared shirt and then looked down at his bearlike frame. "Plus, I kinda stick out."

"Oh." Cory *had* noticed kids staring at him. Like a chump, he'd assumed it was because they knew he was the star running back, come to usher HBS to a future state championship, not because he was a scholarship kid. He looked down and brushed a stray piece of fuzz from his shirt.

The discomfort didn't keep Cory from loading up his tray and thanking the lady at the cash register when she smiled at him and quietly said, "Go ahead. You're all set."

Cory had only taken two steps before another lunch lady called, "Hey, you. Wait!"

He felt his ears burn and knew it had been too good to be true. He had no money, and now he'd have to put all the food back. He looked from the crowded line of other middle school students to the lunch lady.

"You didn't get ice cream," she said, pointing at a freezer case. "Kids should eat ice cream."

Gant nodded at Cory. He had two ice-cream sandwiches on his own tray.

"Sure," Cory said, taking just one. "Thanks."

He followed Gant to the end of a long table and sat down across from his big friend before leaning toward him and lowering his voice. "Man, this place is great. All this stuff for free?"

Gant filled his mouth with half a taco, then spoke through the mess. "Well, not really free. You'll earn it. Believe me."

"Doing what?" Cory asked as he began to eat.

Gant shrugged. "Playing football. It's like a job, bro."

"It's just football, Gant," Cory said. "I love football."

"Well, maybe when you're not in the trenches, it's more like a beach party," Gant said, "but for us hogs it's a grind."

The two of them did little talking after that, mostly because Gant was an eating machine.

Cory had just finished his last bite of ice-cream sandwich and was licking his fingers when Cheyenne appeared out of nowhere. "Hey, little brother. Hey, Gant, you taking care of this cute guy?"

Cory sat, frozen. Over and over, quickly, he repeated the words "no big deal no big deal no big deal" in his mind.

He looked up at Cheyenne, trying not to let his eyes glitter. "Hey."

"What ho? He speaketh. Not shy is he." She grinned at him.

Cory wanted to say that she was the one who hadn't said a word at breakfast or during the ride to school, but instead he told himself, "Nobigdealnobigdealnobigdeal." When he glanced around and saw no sign of Mike, he decided to be bold.

He looked into those big blue eyes and said, "*To be or not to be, that is the question.*"

Cheyenne raised an eyebrow. "Thou speaketh the language of the true bard?"

Cory thought the true bard might be Shakespeare, but he wasn't certain, so he shrugged like it was no big deal either way.

Her face glowed. "Ah, *'brevity is the soul of wit.'* He's doing good hanging out with you, Gant. I know he didn't get it from my brother. That boy's dumb as a rock. See you at dinner, Pollywog."

She mussed Cory's hair and disappeared.

"That girl is a nuclear bomb." Gant followed her with his eyes.

"Eh." Cory spit out the sound and shrugged, inspired now to act completely cool.

"Eh? *Eh?* Are you *crazy?*" Gant leaned across the table and lowered his voice. "She was in my first-period class and the guys were all talking about her. She *already* got asked by a high school kid to the freshman dance. And I'd guess there isn't a guy in this middle school who wouldn't walk through fire to hold her hand, and you say, *'Eh'?*"

"She called me a pollywog, Gant. You think I'm gonna make a statue of her?"

"She noticed you, bro. You're on her radar. She called you *cute.*" Gant huffed. "Then you quoted . . . who? The whole thing was like a scene on the Disney Channel."

"I'm here to play football," Cory said. "Not that stuff."

"Oh." Gant raised his eyebrows. "Mike scare you off? He's pretty tough, but nothing for a guy from the Westside, right?"

"I'm not worried about him, or her," Cory said.

"Well . . ." Gant seemed deeply disappointed, but then he brightened. "I get the football part, though. Today's the day, huh? You ready?"

"Yeah." Cory did his best to sound bored. "I'm all about the games, though."

"Well, perfect practice makes perfect. That's what my Liverpool coach used to say anyway."

The bell rang and they got up to go, parting ways in the hall outside Cory's math class. They wouldn't see each other again until study hall before practice, so Gant gave him a fist bump. "See you out there, bro. Man, I can't wait to see you with your dancing shoes on."

"Dancing shoes?"

"Your cleats, Cor. I heard you got the moves. You're the Touchdown Kid."

Gant's words haunted Cory for the rest of the day because he'd spent that last three years hearing about how he'd never be a football player. Then, against the Falcons, after Liam got hurt, he'd exploded. All he had thought about was *getting* to HBS after Coach McMahan had cast a spell on his mom. What he hadn't really thought about was if he could actually *do* what he'd done in that game more than once. How long would people be calling him Touchdown Kid if he didn't keep scoring touchdowns? He knew the answer: not long.

Those were the thoughts troubling his mind when he walked into the locker room before practice and bumped smack-dab into a much bigger problem.

The sour smell of dried pee and sweat hung low in the warm air.

Mike Chester puffed up his chest and stepped across the tile floor toward Cory, blocking his path. "Nobody told you?"

"Told me what?" Cory tried to sound tough and uncaring at the same time.

"Newbies don't get to use the main entrance to the locker room." Mike wore a wicked grin. "Newbies gotta come in through the bathroom, cuz newbies all smell like poop. And you're our newbie, aren't you?"

Cory looked around. The rest of the kids had all stopped picking out their lockers to stare at the confrontation. Jimbo was nowhere in sight, but when Cory caught Gant's eye, his big new friend stepped forward.

"Okay, Mike, you made your point. He's a newbie." Gant

reached for Cory's arm to pull him along, but quick as a blink Mike flicked a hand, chopping Gant's arm down and away.

"Don't look at me like that, Gant." Mike raised his hands in a karate stance. "I'll strike you five times in the face before you can even *think* about taking a swing."

Cory's chest flooded with adrenaline and joy at the butt kicking that was about to rain down on Mike Chester, but to his surprise, Gant dropped his hands.

In that same moment, Mike made his move.

Mike used the flat of his hand and gave Cory what looked like a shove but felt like a punch. Cory heard the wind leave his body in a powerful gust.

"Huh!"

He stumbled backward with pinwheeling arms and rubbery legs. He glanced off the corner of some lockers and lurched sideways. His foot hit something slick and flew out from under him. In a desperate attempt to stay off the floor, he planted one leg at an awkward angle, twisting his foot. He didn't fall, but a stab of pain lit up his ankle.

Before anything else could happen, a whistle blasted from the other end of the locker room. A butterball of a man with thinning red hair marched in. His coaching gear and visor were in school colors.

"All right! All right!" The coach marched into their midst,

white socks pulled up to his knees, oblivious to any trouble. "You cupcakes should all have your lockers picked out by now. If not, find one, take a lock and get it on. Five minutes and I want everyone in the gym for his equipment. We'll get geared up and get to business. *Business*, boys, that's why we're here."

The coach stopped in front of Cory and the whistle dropped from his mouth as he set a basket of padlocks down on the nearest bench. "Cory Marco, Touchdown Kid? Not here, you're not. Here, you're the newbie. I'm Coach Phipps. Good to have you."

Coach Phipps squinted and eyed Cory from head to toe. "Not much to look at, but Coach McMahan says you're a thoroughbred running back, and if Coach McMahan says it, it's gospel."

Cory shook the coach's hand, surprised at how small it was. Mike had melted into the crowd. Cory stiffened his leg to keep from moving the ankle, telling himself he just needed to walk it off.

He took a padlock like everyone else, found an empty locker next to Gant, and memorized the combination. As he followed the crowd into the gym, he couldn't keep from hobbling. The sharp pain in his ankle wasn't going away. Cory thought of the Westside and Jo-Lonn Dunbar. People said he'd played football one time with a big toe swollen to the size of a hard-boiled egg. Cory needed to be tough, so he bit the inside of his mouth and did his best not to limp.

There were two more sixth-grade coaches in the gym, each standing before several piles of equipment. They looked like they were fresh out of college, with crew cuts and athletic

124

builds. The players filed through cafeteria-style, selecting items that fit from the piles. Cory asked Gant about the coaches.

"The shorter one is Coach Bean," Gant said, "and the big guy is Coach Tackitt. They're both pretty hard-core, but Tackitt is with the linemen. Bean's not so bad. Hey, you okay? You look like you're limping."

"I'm good. Just tweaked my ankle a little." Cory lowered his voice so only Gant could hear him. "That Mike Chester is an idiot. I thought you were gonna pound him."

"I got two words for you." Gant knit his dark eyebrows together and kept his voice down too. "Aidan Brown."

"Aidan Brown?"

"Aidan Brown," Gant repeated. "You know the scholarship we got? The one Liam was supposed to get? You know who got it in sixth grade last year?"

"Aidan Brown? Who is he?" Cory asked.

"Who *was* he, you mean," Gant whispered. "Scholarship kid from some trailer park out in Elbridge. Fast as greased lightning, but he got caught shoplifting and . . ." Gant drew a thumb across his own throat.

"Shoplifting?"

"At Wegmans, the supermarket. Pack of gum. Then he got hurt and that was it. Gone, baby."

"They just kicked him to the curb for a pack of gum?" Cory looked around at all the HBS boys surrounding him with their fancy haircuts and polo shirts.

"I wouldn't say that," Gant said. "They got him a lawyer and everything. Then he got hurt, pulled a hamstring. Lost his confidence. Lost a step. Stopped scoring touchdowns."

"What's that got to do with Mike?" Cory asked, still whispering.

"You or me do something wrong *and* we get hurt or start playing bad? Bro, we are gonzo. No scholarships. No fancy homes. It's just like Monopoly: do not pass Go, do not collect two hundred dollars." Gant shuffled forward in the line before turning his attention back to Cory. "I got my sights set on *the* Ohio State University. A short stop there before I line up for the Patriots, bro. This is my ticket, and if I gotta let some cheese brain like Mike Chester think he's tough, I'm doing it, and you do the same, you hear me? Stay in line, and stay healthy."

It made Cory sullen. "Yeah. I hear you," he said.

There were over thirty boys on the team, and Cory and Gant were in the back part of the pack. He saw Jimbo at the very front, presumably getting the newest pieces of equipment. Mike wasn't far behind. After Jimbo had filled his arms up with equipment, he came walking back toward the locker room under his pile of stuff. He stopped in front of Cory, scowling.

"You shoulda blasted that jerk." Jimbo angled his head back toward the front where Mike was trying on helmets.

"Why didn't *you*?" Cory asked. "I didn't even know you were there."

"I saw. Everyone did." Jimbo glanced at Chester. "He wouldn't try something like that with *me*, that much I promise you."

"Yeah, well . . ." Cory stopped talking. He wanted to say if he had a rich dad who was a big booster, Mike wouldn't have bothered him either, but that would only make Jimbo mad.

"Anyway, you better get some paybacks when we get out on the field," Jimbo said. "Everyone will be watching to see if you lay into him or wimp out."

"I'll knock down whoever I have to." Cory shifted some weight onto his ankle, testing it. A jolt of pain rocketed through the joint. Cory bit his lip.

"Good. That's what I like to hear."

Cory made his way through the line. He got some decent pants with thigh and knee pads that looked almost new. The rib pads looked a little run down, and by the time he got to the helmets, all that was left was junk. He looked at Gant, who had the only giant helmet in the bunch, and it looked like it was in pretty good shape.

"They had to special order this bad boy last season." Gant clunked the bucket-sized helmet down on his head. "It's the latest and greatest, a Riddell Revolution."

Cory shrugged and found a scratched and battered silver helmet that at least fit him. Coach Phipps was helping another kid get his helmet adjusted, and when he turned and looked at Cory, he scowled. "How come you're all the way at the end of the line?"

Cory blinked at him and opened his mouth to speak, but nothing came out.

"It's a good lesson." Coach Phipps frowned. "You snooze, you lose. You're here to be a leader, Marco, not a latecomer at the end of the line."

Cory could nearly taste his coach's disgust in the air and it made his stomach turn.

"Now I gotta do something I was hoping not to have to do, but you leave me no choice, son. Come with me." Coach Phipps turned and stomped across the gym.

Cory followed, preparing himself for the unknown punishment.

Coach Phipps marched straight into his office, where a tall brown box stood next to his desk. He glanced back at Cory. His round red face was now pinched and his nostrils widened. "What are you limping for?"

"I'm not." Cory stumbled on his own words. "I . . . I slipped. Something on the locker room floor. I'm fine."

"You better be," Coach Phipps said. "You know how much one of these full rides is worth? Forty thousand a year, times seven years. Over a quarter-million dollars. You thought about that yet?"

Cory shook his head. "No." It was a scary number.

"Which is why I can't have you lagging behind everyone. You need to be first in everything, or darn close." Coach Phipps reached into the box and took out a shiny silver helmet wrapped in plastic and handed it to Cory. "You can't be our top running

129

back and have some garbage helmet. Here, give me that. I try to save a couple new helmets in case one of the old ones gets busted during the season. Now there's only one left. I've got to order more. Does it fit?"

It was beautiful, a Riddell Revolution. Cory unwrapped it and put it on. It felt smooth and cool and comfortable. "Awesome."

"Yeah," Coach Phipps said. "And you better play that way—awesome."

Forcing himself to walk straight, Cory returned to the gym for the rest of his gear and then headed for the locker room, where Gant was already half-dressed.

"Look." Cory showed him the Revolution.

Gant gave him a fist bump. "Big time, bro. You and me."

Cory dressed quickly. Gant helped him and together they marched out of the locker room. They were crossing some blacktop next to the tennis courts on their way to the football fields when Cory heard a noise moving up fast behind him like no other. He spun around and saw two columns of full-grown football players crunching the pavement beneath their cleats like some grinding machine. As they crunched, they chanted in one low voice.

"*H-B-S . . . H-B-S . . . H-B-S . . .*"

Cory and Gant stepped aside and the engine of legs and feet crunched past them, twisting around the corner and continuing out onto the grass before disappearing down a hillside.

"The varsity." Gant stared in awe. "You see the size of them?"

"We'll be them someday," Cory said, sounding confident.

He just hoped his ankle would hold up.

He and Gant jogged out onto the middle school field, where the seventh-grade team was already finishing up. The school staggered the end times for the high and middle schools and queued up the different football squads in the library for study hall. There were three football fields spread out below for six teams in all to share: sixth, seventh, eighth, freshman, JV, and the varsity that had just stomped past them. Like the cogs of a complex machine, the teams rotated around the fields, study hall, and locker rooms in complete synchronization. Everything was timed to the minute.

The air was warm and moist, and Cory could smell the dirt beneath the grass. Thick clouds crowded the sky and seemed too heavy to move in the still air. Cory struggled not to limp, but his ankle was now throbbing, and he wondered if it wasn't something serious. He had to keep going, though. Coach Phipps's words rang clearly in his mind.

Mike Chester was off by himself with a football tucked under his arm, running along the goal line, bursting forth, then cutting right, left, then right again before lining up and going back the way he'd come. He was already showboating for the top spot.

Cory swallowed and his mouth got dry. He didn't think there was any way in the world he could cut like that.

Coach Phipps blew the whistle and the team ran to the end zone, forming eight lines without being told. Cory followed the pack, then remembered Coach Phipps's demand that he get to the front. He stepped ahead of Jimbo.

"Hey!" Jimbo gave him a shove.

"Help me out, Jimbo." Cory tried not to sound too desperate. "Coach told me to get into the front of every line if I wanted to keep my scholarship."

Jimbo laughed, then said, "Okay, but tomorrow you cut someone else or get here first. I'm not your punk."

To Cory's surprise, Jimbo moved to the next line and shoved Parker back so he could be first there. Warm-ups began, and Cory struggled just to jog through the high-knee drills and the sideways shuffle runs. No one seemed to notice, though. Spirits were high, and many of the players hooted and howled and slapped each other's shoulder pads in the excitement of a new season. Football for Cory was already a month old. He would have been like a fish in a pond if it weren't for his aching ankle.

Warm-ups turned into agility drills. Cory was awful and quickly broke out in a sweat, more from pain than from exercise. When the team broke down into offensive individual work, Cory went with Coach Phipps and the rest of the running backs and quarterbacks. Coach Bean joined them with his bunch of wide receivers. The group of skill players followed Coach Phipps on an easy jog over to a spot on the field near the fifty-yard line. When they got there, Coach gave Cory a look, then blew his whistle, pointed to a spot next to an orange cone, and said, "Okay, go routes, give me one line right here!"

Cory jumped forward, knowing the coach wanted him to be first in line. His ankle barked with pain. He saw a flash of movement, ignored the pain, and beat Mike Chester to the spot.

He never expected what happened next.

Mike Chester started to walk away.

Cory breathed a sigh of relief, but it had no sooner left his body than Mike spun around and blasted Cory with a forearm, knocking him back so that he could stand at the front of the line.

Cory saw red.

He didn't think. He reacted.

The Westside *was* a tough place, and Cory knew what it was like to be in a fight on the practice field. He didn't have to plan to grab Mike's face mask; he just did it. Yanking his new teammate forward and down, Cory clubbed the side of Mike's helmet twice to ring his bell. Giving him a final yank, Cory sidestepped Chester's flying form, tripping him as he went past.

Cory stepped up to the cone and looked back at Mike, ready if he came at him again. Chester sprang up, and Cory saw a hate-filled face that reminded him of Dirty's face after his mom had slapped the older boy down.

Cory knew it wasn't over, and he lowered his center to be ready. As Mike screamed and launched himself, Coach Phipps stepped in and shoved him sideways. Mike tipped and went down again.

"Enough!" The coach was red faced and growling. "You wanna be first in line, Chester? You gotta hustle. You snooze, you lose. Now get back to the end!"

Jimbo and Parker had positioned themselves off to the side. Coach Phipps tossed Jimbo a ball. "Let 'em fly, Jimbo."

Jimbo held the ball out in front of him with both hands as though he were taking a snap from the center. "Go route, Cory. Set, hike!"

Cory took off down the sideline toward the end zone on a go route, forgetting all about the pain in his ankle. He was soaring with adrenaline and joy. It felt so good to have Coach Phipps put Mike Chester in his place—and Cory had seen the looks of admiration and wonder from his teammates after he'd tossed his rival to the ground. Thirty yards down the field, Jimbo's pass arced above him, floating through the air like a wingless bird in the gray sky, then dropping quickly toward the grass.

Cory raced under it, hands outstretched, pulled it in, and dashed across the goal line.

"That's the business!" Coach Phipps screamed. "That's how it's done, you cupcakes. Now, give me more!"

Cory swelled with pride.

But even as he jogged back up the sideline toward the back

of the line, his ankle began pounding like a drum, and he realized he'd be standing directly behind Mike Chester.

Mike didn't look at Cory, though, and he didn't say a word. They ran other routes before the receivers jogged off with Coach Bean.

Cory stayed on edge, ready for the whistle and determined to get to the front of the line for the next drill, whatever that might be. Next was a handoff drill, quarterbacks taking make-believe snaps, pivoting, and practicing the exchange with the running backs. Cory got to the front of that, too, despite his ankle, but when that drill ended and Coach Phipps pointed to a new spot for a cut drill, Mike beat him.

Cory looked at the coach as he slipped in behind Mike. Phipps was chuckling to himself, and it made Cory mad that he seemed to enjoy the bad blood between two of his players. The cut drill was a zigzagging run back and forth between cones spread out over thirty yards. Coach Phipps got at the end of the cones and took out his stopwatch.

"Okay, you wanna see playing time on this squad? You gotta be able to cut, and cut fast, quarterbacks too. Best time last year was a 9.7. If you can't break 11.5, you're probably gonna end up with Coach Tackitt and his hogs. Mike! You been chirping at me how good you are, son. Let's see it. Ready . . ."

Mike got down in his stance and Coach Phipps closed one eye and held up his stopwatch. "When you're ready . . ."

Mike sucked in a deep breath and bolted out of his stance. He reached the first cone, planted his foot, and exploded back the other way. Back and forth he went, air blasting from his mouth like some crazy piston. As he stretched through the

135

finish line, he cried out with an angry growl.

Coach Phipps studied his watch. "Not bad. Not bad at all, 10.3. Okay, Scholarship, let's see what you got!"

Cory's insides melted. Whatever he really had, he sure didn't have right now. He could barely jog without hobbling. Cutting like this—if he could even do it—would be painful and difficult and slow.

"Let's go! Get down! We ain't got all day, Marco!"

Cory looked back. Jimbo squinted with impatience. He looked in front of him. Chester jogged back toward the line with a smug grin. Cory gritted his teeth and got down in his stance.

"When you're ready!" the coach shouted.

Cory took off.

The first cut was on his left ankle and it was fine. He seemed to be moving okay straight ahead, despite the pain. When he hit the next cone and planted on his bad ankle, he cried out, but kept going, back and forth, back and forth, working his way toward his coach with uncontrollable tears filling his eyes.

He burst past the coach and stopped, turning to look.

Coach Phipps examined the time on his watch.

Cory tried to read his face, but it was an empty page.

Coach Phipps looked up from his watch wearing an expression of disbelief and disgust. "You sure you're the same kid Coach McMahan's been bragging on? The *Touchdown* Kid? You just ran a 12.7. My grandmother could do better than that. I just gave you a new Revolution helmet, son. I may have to take that back. You couldn't run through a kindergarten class moving like that."

Cory grabbed his leg. "My ankle, Coach."

"Your *ankle*?" Coach Phipps cussed under his breath and barked out a laugh. "When you *slipped*? In the locker room? On a bar of soap or something?"

"Something on the floor." Cory's face burned with shame. It was a private conversation, but he knew his teammates were listening.

Coach Phipps looked past Cory, ignoring him. "Who's up?

Muiller? Let's go, son. Get in your stance."

Cory hobbled back to the line. After each player had gone, Coach Phipps blew his whistle and shouted for the entire team to take a water break. Cory followed the pack toward the water horse, a plastic pipe on legs that was attached to a hose and spouted a dozen streams of water. Cory sucked some down. Wiping his mouth, he turned to find Jimbo standing there with a frown.

"Come on, Cory," Jimbo said. "You gotta suck it up, man. Don't start out behind the eight ball."

"This thing is killing me, Jimbo." Cory hated the sound of his own voice.

Jimbo only shook his head and harshly whispered, "Suck it up. It's a tough game. You ran that go route just fine, then you start limping around?"

Cory bit his lip. He wanted to smack Jimbo more than he wanted to explain that he suspected he had sprained his ankle. "Just forget it."

Cory pushed past him, looking for Gant, but by the time the big lineman disconnected himself from the water horse, Coach Phipps was blowing his whistle and shouting. "Okay! Give me a first-team offense in a pro set right here on the ball!"

Cory took off for the spot on the field where his coach stood. As he got closer, he saw Coach Phipps watching him. The frown he wore slowed Cory's pace. The closer he got, the less certain he was about his status. Linemen were getting in their spots on the line. Cory saw pushing and shoving between them from the corner of his eye. No one contested Gant's spot at left tackle. Jimbo fell in behind the center, with Garrison

Green falling immediately in behind him at the fullback spot. Coach Phipps's look seemed to be warning Cory away. The words about him not being what Coach McMahan said made Cory think twice. Just as he reached the place where the tailback should be, Mike Chester jumped in front of him.

Cory's hesitation cost him the spot. He stopped and considered bumping Mike out of his place, maybe even fighting him for it, but the look on Coach Phipps's face gave him no encouragement. He paused for another moment before walking to a spot in the grass where a horizontal line of kids was forming to watch. Cory fell into the ranks. If the Coach wanted him with the first team, he'd put him there.

His heart lifted as Coach Phipps marched his way, and Cory waited—along with the rest of the team—for the coach to speak.

"I thought I was clear with you, Marco, what I said over there."
Coach Phipps narrowed his small eyes.

"The part about not running through a kindergarten class?"
Cory said.

Laughter erupted from his teammates all around.

Coach Phipps sneered at Cory. "You think this is a joke?"

"No, Coach."

"I told you 'be first,' but you don't want to be first, do you?"
The coach's voice was boiling.

"No," Cory said. "I do, Coach."

"Did you or did you not just now let Chester jump right in
front of you?" His voice grew louder.

"I thought you wanted me to let him," Cory said, the world
slipping away on him, "the way you looked at me and what you
said in the cut drill."

"Did I not tell you to be *first*?" Coach Phipps shouted. "Get out of my sight! Go! Run a lap, son. Run *ten laps*! Winners never quit and quitters never win!"

Cory hesitated, wondering if the coach was serious. Things had come so far unraveled, he felt like he was back at Westside with Coach Mellon instead of the star recruit come to help win a championship one day.

"Go!" Coach Phipps screamed, his small eyes popping like a bug's.

Cory limped off and began a slow, steady jog around the field. He tried to watch what was happening as he went, but the confusion of bodies and whistles and players running to and fro was too hard to follow. Sweat was streaming down his face and stinging his eyes.

Cory was running along the back side of the end zone, huffing and hurting, when Mike Chester took a toss on a sweep play, juked out two defenders, and dashed into the end zone.

Chester held the ball up for him to see. "I told you this spot is mine. Why don't you go back to the slums where you belong?"

Hatred torched Cory's heart, but he didn't even have the energy to reply.

Finally, he lapped the field for the tenth time and took his place with the rest of the backup players in their line across the field behind the team drill. Cory hadn't even caught his breath before Coach Phipps blasted his whistle and hollered for them all to line up on the fifty-yard line for ladder runs.

Cory found Gant. "Ladder *runs*? Like, more than one? How many?"

Gant was huffing too after having been in the thick of the action all practice long. Sweat glazed his face, and he shook his head. "I heard Coach P likes ladders the way a pig likes mud."

Coach P liked ladders *more* than a pig likes mud.

They ran until three kids barfed, with vomit exploding from their face masks as they staggered to the sideline. Cory's ankle shrieked and he had to swallow down the remnants of his own lunch as he staggered into the bunch of players crowding around their coach after the last ladder. He dropped to a knee like the rest of them.

"Okay, not too bad today." Coach P sounded like he was admitting to a crime. "But tomorrow we gotta get down to some real business. Make sure you cupcakes get plenty of water and plenty of rest. This ain't gonna get any easier, I can promise you that."

No one groaned. No one blinked. Cory already knew it was the HBS way. For his part, he bit his lip and hobbled to the locker room. Inside his backpack was the TracFone, waiting like an escape pod on some alien spaceship. All he needed to do was call. His mom had said any place, any time. Cory shed his shoulder pads and opened his locker. He removed the phone from his backpack and turned it over in his fingers like a smooth stone.

When he felt a tap on his shoulder, he spun around.

Mike Chester stood there, glowering at Cory with a small group of frowning players behind him. They were stripped down to their football pants and cleats, bare chested, like cannibal warriors from a movie.

"Okay, newbie," Mike said. "Time to sing."

37

"Go ahead," a big lineman with a face like a frying pan said, "sing."

A crooked smile wormed its way onto Cory's face because this was obviously some kind of a joke. He didn't know yet if the joke would be funny or cruel. By the look on his rival's face, he suspected cruel. Cory looked across the locker room to Gant. His giant friend was smiling too, and that gave Cory some hope.

"What do you mean?" Cory asked.

"Sing," Mike said.

"Sing what?" Cory said. He had been in third grade when even his loving mother said he was tone-deaf and couldn't carry a tune. "I can't sing."

"Everyone sings. It's a tradition. Just do it, Cory."

All heads turned because it was Jimbo talking now, and he looked annoyed.

Cory set down his phone and gestured with both hands, appealing to Jimbo. "Yeah, but I really can't. I'm tone-deaf. It's awful. It's not even singing."

"That's even better." Mike broke into an evil smile. "Newbies are supposed to entertain us."

"Well, I'm not singing." Cory turned back to his locker and stripped off his own sweaty T-shirt. No one behind him moved. The entire locker room was frozen, waiting. Cory turned back.

"Sing, or we give you a swirly. You choose." Mike chuckled. "It's a tradition."

"Swirly?" Cory wrinkled his face.

"Yeah," Mike laughed. "A swirly. We put your head in the toilet and flush it."

"Cory, can't you just sing?" Gant spoke quietly and Cory knew there was no way out. No one was helping him.

Still, he wasn't going to sing.

"No," Cory said.

Chester shrugged and looked behind him at the big linemen. "Okay, swirly it is."

Mike Chester and his goons slowly came at him.

"Swir-lee, swir-lee, swir-lee." The chant began low, then it started to grow. *"Swir-lee, swir-lee, swir-lee!"*

Cory looked around. The entire team was closing in on him like a zombie apocalypse. He'd fight, though. He wasn't going to make it easy on them.

They began to reach out for him, fingers extended and slowly clawing the air.

If he was truthful with himself later on, he'd have to admit that it was Cheyenne who prompted him to do what he did.

The thought of her hearing of his ridiculous voice—making a fool of himself—or worse yet, being dunked and flushed in a dirty toilet, was too much. He was desperate enough to do just about anything, even something crazy. Something dangerous.

And that's what he did.

He knew Mike Chester was the leader.

Cory looked him in the eye and snarled with a full dose of hatred. "You touch me and you'll wish you didn't."

The sound that came out of Cory's mouth was so nasty he startled everyone, even himself. The players froze.

Mike forced a laugh. "Oh yeah? What are *you* gonna do? There's thirty of us."

"I'm gonna fight you tooth and nail," Cory said. "But that's no big deal. You guys'll get me. It's what's gonna happen to you afterward . . ."

Cory knew he had everyone's undivided attention. "Remember Liam? The guy who was gonna be here until he got hurt?"

"What's he gonna do?" Mike laughed for real now.

"Not him." Cory shook his head and clucked his tongue.

"His brother and his brother's friends—they're my friends too—bad, bad dudes. Westside? You want a taste of the *Westside*? Our rules: a bunch of softies from the suburbs jumps a Westsider? It's payback time. I just hope Dirty doesn't cut you up. Dirty, that's his name; he loves his knife."

Hands dropped.

People stepped back.

"Yeah, right." Mike scoffed, but the glimmer in his eyes had been snuffed out and his laughter sounded like it came from a can. "I don't even believe you. Dirty. Sounds like a cartoon."

Cory shrugged. "Fine. I'll tell him you said that. He'll like that, you calling him a cartoon. He'll have a laugh. You can have a laugh together."

"C'mon, guys." Mike looked around at the fading crowd. "He's lying. He can't stop all of us. He's gotta sing. Newbies always gotta sing. Or they swirl."

Cory knew the tide had turned in his favor, but it wasn't over yet. "Yeah, all of a sudden nobody wants to get unzipped by a combat knife. It's just you, Mike. No swirly. No singing. You'll have to listen to your iTunes."

Cory turned his back to them all and began to stow his equipment. Tension crackled in the warm, stuffy locker room air. The ripe smell of sweat was especially sour.

Cory pretended not to care, but he couldn't help cringing as he waited for Mike Chester to either walk away or punch him in the back of the head.

"Fine," Mike said. "You don't have to sing, Marco, you jerk. You stink anyway, and probably won't be here in two weeks. Meantime, don't think you're *really* on this team, 'cuz you're not."

Mike walked away and the locker room quietly came back to life. Cory's heart went from a sprint to a jog and his breath came back. By the time he'd changed back into his clothes, people were looking past him or through him, and he realized what Chester said was true—he wasn't part of it anymore. Even as a fifth-string running back with the Cougars, he'd been part of the team, laughing and joking. Grinning and groaning and trying to top Liam's imitations of Coach Mellon and the way he'd scratch his butt crack when he thought no one was looking.

Now, suddenly, Cory was a ghost. He thought about just

getting up on the bench and belting out "The Star-Spangled Banner." He would have, except for everything else that had happened to him already. He couldn't break his last thread of dignity. Embarrassing himself would be too much to take, and Cheyenne would snicker at him along with the rest. How could she not?

He pretended to be busy at his locker until Gant closed his with a crash. Cory hurried to catch up—hobbling in pain—as Gant left the locker room. They walked a ways down the empty hallway before Cory spoke. "Bunch of bull, right? Singing?"

"Yeah." Gant shrugged, but Cory could tell he was out of sorts.

"I mean, you can probably sing," Cory said. "I mean, if you can sing, that's another thing, but I'd be making a fool of myself."

"Yeah." Gant made the word walk the plank, forcing it from his mouth.

"You think I'm wrong?" Cory tugged on his arm.

Gant pulled away. "Come on. Let's not talk here."

Gant took off, walking briskly out the door and stopping in the shade of the tennis court fence. The ball thumped off their racquets as the kids volleyed it back and forth, grunting like weight lifters.

Gant looked back as if he would be embarrassed to be seen talking with Cory. "You're new. Everyone does it. Sings. Plus, you're hurt before you even get on the field?"

"You saw me slip." Cory tried not to sound desperate. "That idiot Chester *pushed* me. What if I tell Coach P *that*?"

Panic flooded Gant's face. He shook his head wildly. "Don't.

You don't do that, Cory. This isn't just about you. I'm a scholarship kid too. You got to fit in. This is the rich man's world."

Cory huffed.

Gant continued. "Bro, you can pretend all you want, but you come from the Westside. You talk like it. No father. Free lunch. Some guy named Dirty cuttin' people?"

A tennis ball smashed into the chain-link fence, and one of the players hollered like he'd scored a touchdown.

"See?" Gant smirked. "You see kids playing *tennis* in your old school?"

Cory did see. "Even if I could sing—which I really can't—I can't do it now, Gant. If I do it now, no one respects me. They'll say Chester punked me. I can't do it. Not for anyone."

Gant sucked in his lower lip and nodded. "Yeah, but lay low now, okay? No more trouble, right, bro? You gotta get that ankle well and do your Adrian Peterson dance—runnin' people over and all that Touchdown Kid stuff. Was that for real? That's how they talked about you."

Cory actually doubted himself. How had he ever exploded on the football field? But it had to be true. "Coach McMahan was the one who started calling me the Touchdown Kid. I just did my thing."

"Yeah." Gant scrunched up his forehead. "That's the good part, Coach McMahan. He's the god of football, and that'll keep you alive until you stop limping. Till then, though, keep cool with Chester and everyone else. Just get along!"

"I don't want any trouble, Gant." Cory shook his head. "But those jumping beans you got?"

Gant patted his pocket with pride. "Yeah?"

150

Cory frowned. "That's like us, Gant."

Gant removed the two beans from his pocket, held them in his palm, and wrinkled his brow. "Say what?"

"We're trapped," Cory said. "And we gotta jump to make people happy. We stop jumping? It's over. We're done."

"Hey." Gant poked at one of the beans with his finger while the other one jiggled around in the cup of his hand. "I think this one's shot too."

"See?" Cory said. "That's what I'm talking about, Gant. Now what? You dump that thing in the nearest trash can."

"You some lawyer?" Gant said. "Stop makin' everything so complicated. They're jumpin' beans. Besides, this one might come back. Maybe it's just sleepin'."

Cory saw Jimbo pop out of the school, looking around for him. In the parking lot, he saw Mrs. Muiller's Range Rover roll up. "I gotta go."

"Wait." Gant stopped him. "I got an idea."

"An idea?"

"Maybe a way to fix this whole thing."

Jimbo was waving to him now, and Cory held up a finger signaling he'd be right there. "Tell me, Gant. Tell me quick."

Football players of all shapes and sizes drained steadily from the back entrance of the school. Cars lined up along the parking lot and around the corner. They'd snake close, gobble up a kid or two, and then surge away. The gleaming black Range Rover moved to the front of the pack. Jimbo loaded his backpack into the SUV and waved at Cory again with both hands.

"Gant?"

Gant looked like he was still thinking. His eyes widened. "She likes you. She can help."

"Who?" Cory wrinkled his face. "Jimbo's mom?"

"His sister. Cheyenne."

"You want me to ask Cheyenne to do what, protect me from Mike Chester? I can fight my own fights, Gant."

Gant shook his big, shaggy head. "Just help. She's got Mike on a short leash. I saw him talking to her after the last bell. ,

Dude was cow eyed and purrin' like a kitten, but I know she likes you. I saw that in lunch."

"Like a sister." Cory tried to control his own heartbeat.

Gant shrugged. "Sister, girlfriend, whatever. She *likes* you, Cor. I know it. She can help. You just explain it all. She'll figure something out. Girls are like that, especially these rich girls. They're used to gettin' what they want."

Mrs. Muiller tooted the Ranger Rover's horn.

"You're crazy, Gant." Cory took off, limping fast.

"Trust me!" Gant hollered after him. "Forget about jumping beans. Just do it!"

Jimbo gave Cory a cold look and slid into the front seat. Cory took his place in the back.

"We can't hold up the line," Mrs. Muiller complained as she took off, adding some lipstick and angling the rearview mirror to check the job as she sped away. "Jimbo, that's on you."

"Me?" Jimbo's jaw slid sideways.

"Yes, Cory is our guest. He's part of the family. The football family . . . and our family too." She flicked aside a lock of brassy blond hair and flashed Cory a huge red smile.

Jimbo crossed his arms and harrumphed.

"What's that look?" his mom asked.

"Nothing."

"How was practice?" She sounded like a songbird, hitting the high notes.

Jimbo shook his head.

She adjusted the mirror so she could lock her own blue eyes on Cory. "Cory?"

"Not great," Cory said.

Jimbo snorted. "I'll say."

"I hurt my ankle." It was the best Cory could offer.

"Oh, my." Mrs. Muiller switched on the radio. "This sport. 'Ice and Advil'—that's what my daddy always said. You'll heal."

She turned up the volume, sparing Cory the need to reply.

Back at the house, Jimbo disappeared. Mrs. Muiller gave Cory a bag of ice and two Advil. "Get around these. Did you get your homework done in study hall? I love that study hall for you boys."

"I did," Cory said, "but I thought I'd go over some notes and read ahead. They gave us *The Outsiders*."

"Notes? Reading ahead? You sound like Cheyenne." Mrs. Muiller put her hand to her mouth and hollered toward the stairs, "Cory's reading ahead, Jimbo! You hear!"

Cory wondered if things could get worse.

"*The Outsiders* . . . I think we read that in school too." She chewed her lower lip.

"Yeah," Cory said. "So far it's not that good."

"And you're reading ahead anyway." She clucked her tongue. "Well, get that ice on your ankle. School's important, but so is football—at least around here it is . . . Dinner at seven."

Cory retreated downstairs to his room. He wondered where Cheyenne was and had a wild hope that she'd be sitting there like she'd been last night. When he opened the door, though, the room was quiet and empty. Cory sat on the bed, laid the ice bag over his ankle, and picked the book out of his backpack.

He had settled in, his ankle aching like a bad tooth from the cold, when he heard the faint titter of girls laughing outside his window. Then, something else . . . a splash?

He limped to the window.

Through the leafy bushes, shadows flickered out by the pool. Another splash, then more laughing. He left his room and limped down the hall, crossing the game room before silently opening the glass door. The shrieks intensified, laughter swirling with delight like some new flavored ice cream. It drew him out.

Three piles of soccer cleats and uniforms lay on a lounge chair.

He watched Cheyenne and two friends from behind the bushes. They had stripped to their underwear and sports bras and were jumping in and out of the pool, pushing and shoving and laughing. The moment he realized what they were wearing—or what they weren't wearing—Cory leaped for the door. His ankle buckled and he crashed sideways into a glass-topped table and chairs. The table went over. Glass exploded.

Cory lay in stunned silence until the face of a girl he thought he'd seen in math class appeared. She was tall and pretty, with blond hair that was lighter and straighter than Cheyenne's. A thick towel covered everything but her face and skinny legs. He thought her name was Tiffanae.

"Oh my God!" she shrieked. "Creeper!"

Cheyenne appeared, also thickly wrapped. "Cory?"

"I'm outta here, Cheyenne," Tiffanae said.

The third girl appeared and said, "You think he saw us? Wait till Mike finds out."

Cheyenne stood frozen.

A small sliver of glass poked up from Cory's palm like an icicle. A crimson bead of blood swelled, broke, and ran down his wrist. He thought of Liam, still lying in the hospital with a knee destroyed nearly as completely as his dreams, and Cory knew why everything was against him. This wasn't his path. Liam was supposed to be living in this house, hanging around with Gant and Jimbo, playing for HBS, and taking Mike Chester's position.

Cory plucked the shard of glass from his palm and looked up at Cheyenne's face, knowing that the charade—it *was* a charade, a silent, bumbling make-believe—was over.

"Don't be stupid," Cheyenne snapped.

Cory could tell by the looks on the girls' faces that they—like him—weren't sure who Cheyenne was talking to.

Then she turned to the first girl. "Cory *lives* here. He's not a creeper. Don't even start with that, Tiffanae."

"He saw our underwear." Tiffanae poked out her lower lip.

"Big deal. It's like a bathing suit," Cheyenne said. "Get over it. The poor kid is *bleeding*."

"Yeah," said the third girl.

"See?" Cheyenne said. "Tami gets it."

"Okay." Tiffanae shrugged pleasantly, and just like that, Cory was off the hook.

He picked himself up off the ground, dusting glass off himself.

"Be careful. Come on, let me get you a bandage." Cheyenne

reached for his hand, drawing him from the mess. "No, don't touch that glass. Leave it. Helga will get it. What happened?"

"I needed to talk to you." Cory's insides began to unravel. There was so much to say, and he knew she was reading his face with those blue eyes.

"You guys wait for me." She spoke to her friends with the tone of a kind and concerned adult. "I'll be back."

Tiffanae and Tami obeyed without a word, shuffling off to the lounge chairs. Cheyenne brought him back inside the game room. She grabbed a wad of Kleenex and pressed it against his palm. Sitting on the leather couch, her hair damp as seaweed, she asked, "What's going on?"

Cory took a deep breath and told her everything. The only part he left out was where he threatened Chester with Liam's brother and his friends.

When he finished, she nodded to herself, making up her mind. "First, you've got to get better. My dad knows the trainer at SU. You need the best. You can't believe what they did when I sprained my ankle in lacrosse—cold compression boots and electric stim. I was back in a week. Injuries happen."

"Not in the locker room." Cory hung his head. He couldn't help sounding glum.

"It is what it is. And, oh, I'll fix Michael Chester." She spoke bitterly.

He looked up. "I thought . . . well, you like him, right?"

"I *liked* him because he was the underdog, Cory, not the bully." Her eyes flashed angrily, then her face and voice softened together. "I always root for the underdog, Cory. Now—apparently—that's you."

159

Cory was no stranger to being the underdog, so it didn't bother him when Cheyenne pleaded his case to Mr. Muiller at the dinner table.

"That coach is off his rocker." Cheyenne thumped the table and her silverware danced as she turned to her father. "Treating Cory like dirt when he's got a sprained ankle? You wouldn't stand for that if he did it to Jimbo."

Jimbo drank his milk, then glared at her across the table with a white mustache on his lip. Cory knew he wasn't happy about the way things had gone. Jimbo had expected a superstar for a houseguest, and he'd been sulking since he sat down.

"Wait a minute, *what?*" Mr. Muiller sputtered and used one of the fancy cloth napkins to wipe some food from his face. "Coach Phipps put Mike Chester in as the starting halfback? And he didn't send you to Kayla Rice?"

"Who's Kayla?" Cory asked.

"The varsity trainer." Mr. Muiller rose from his seat and turned to Mrs. Muiller. "Did we get a call from Phipps?"

Mrs. Muiller gulped the rest of her wine and started pouring more. "*I* didn't. Howard, sit down and finish your dinner."

"Not until I have a word with Phipps." Mr. Muiller threw his napkin on the table and grabbed his cell phone from the counter between the dining area and kitchen.

"Dad . . ." Jimbo whined. "It's football. Coaches are supposed to be tough."

"Tough, not stupid." Mr. Muiller tapped away at his phone.

"*'Come not between the dragon and his wrath.'*" Cheyenne flashed a fake smile at her brother.

"You can take that Shakespeare and stick it in your ear!" Jimbo burst up out of his seat and pointed at Cory. "He wouldn't even *sing*!"

"Wait, what?" Mr. Muiller stopped dialing. "What do you mean? Everyone sings, right? I sang when I was your age. It's HBS tradition."

Jimbo recounted his version of the story in the locker room after practice. Cory sank down in his seat and pressed on the Band-Aid covering his palm because the cut had begun to ache.

"And then he threatened Mike Chester with some gangster criminal from the Westside who carries a knife." Jimbo looked with great satisfaction at the mask of horror on his mother's face.

"He was being *bullied*!" Cheyenne's chair screeched across the floor as she jumped to her feet. "Everyone was ganging up on him. What was he supposed to do? And what about the swirly? You didn't say that!"

"Swirly?" Mrs. Muiller took another sip of her wine.

"They stick your head in the toilet," Cheyenne said, "then flush it."

"That's disgusting." Mrs. Muiller stopped the wineglass halfway to her lips and winced.

"That's why he said that about the kid with the knife, and he should have." Cheyenne jutted her chin out at her brother.

"How would you know? You weren't there," Jimbo said.

"Because Cory told me. That's how I know."

"You're the one who likes Mike Chester," Jimbo replied.

"In any fight, I like the *under*dog."

"Well you got the underdog with *him*." Jimbo nodded toward Cory. "He looked like a wet dish towel out there."

"All right, *stop!*" Mr. Muiller slammed his palm flat on the table, and everyone did stop. "That's better. Now, Cory, singing isn't a bad thing. It's a tradition. Every fifth-grader does it, and when kids join HBS after that, they're expected to sing. It's harmless."

"Yeah, but I can't sing." Dinner grew suddenly heavy in Cory's stomach. "I'm tone-deaf."

"Tone . . . what?"

Cheyenne spoke right up. "Tone-deaf, Dad. He can't hear the notes. It's ugly when somebody tone-deaf tries to sing."

"Who cares about ugly?" Mr. Muiller scrubbed his blond beard with a free hand. "It's a locker room."

"Please . . ." The rest of what Cory wanted to say got jammed up.

"He's our *guest*," Cheyenne argued.

"Oh, fine. I'll talk to Phipps." The father held up his phone as proof.

"And he's not a dish towel." Cheyenne glared at her brother.

"That's right," Mr. Muiller said. "He's Coach McMahan's recruit, so we already know he's a player. Right, Cory?"

Cory hesitated.

"Of course he's a player." Cheyenne's arms flew about her head. "Coach McMahan said he was the Touchdown Kid."

There was a moment of silence as everyone absorbed the import of Coach McMahan's endorsement. Just the thought of the upright coach made Cory sit a bit straighter. In the back of his mind, he made a note to thank Gant and tell him what a genius he was for telling him to involve Cheyenne.

"I did what I did." Cory spoke hesitantly at first, but then picked up steam. "When Coach McMahan saw me, I ran four touchdowns and two hundred and thirty seven yards! And that was just in the second half."

Mr. Muiller cleared his throat and shot Jimbo a look. "Injuries are part of the game. Jimbo had a bad elbow last season and missed two games. Remember, Jimbo?"

Jimbo bit his lip and looked at his plate, cheeks on fire.

"I'll have a word with Phipps and we'll get you in to see Zach Houlaires. The Syracuse University trainer. Works magic on people." Mr. Muiller left the table with the phone already to his ear.

Cory's hand began to throb. He looked around and knew he could really use some magic.

The rest of dinner was quiet, and Cory finished quickly and returned to the basement.

Alone, in the dark of his room, Cory needed some sympathy.

He sat staring at the wall for nearly an hour, willing Cheyenne to come slipping into his room. He wished she had sensed his need to talk, but nothing happened, and he sure wasn't going to sneak around the enormous house looking for her.

He sighed out loud, then turned on the light and fished the TracFone out of his backpack. He stared at it for a moment and thought about dialing his mom. That was too weak, though. He couldn't cry to his momma. She'd probably freak out and demand he come back home.

Instead, he dialed information and got the number for the hospital.

It took him several minutes, but finally he was patched through to Liam's room. When it began to ring, Cory fought the urge to hang up. It was ten o'clock, probably too late. He readied his finger over the End button, planning to hang up quickly at the sound of Liam's mom's voice.

"Hello?"

"Liam?"

"Hey, Cory! What's up, bud?"

"I was afraid I'd wake you."

"Ha! I sleep all day in this joint," Liam said. "Except for physical therapy. I can barely move this thing, but it still wears me out and they have to pump up my painkillers and I zonk out half the day. I was watching *Criminal Minds*. Reminds me of my brother. Haha."

"How is your brother?"

Liam lowered his voice. "Looks like he beat the Shamrock rap. Everyone knows now that you didn't talk, so . . . that's a good thing."

"Of course I didn't talk. I know better than that," Cory said. "Hey, you're not the only one needing rehab anymore."

"You're hurt?" Liam's voice was filled with real concern. "Is it bad?"

"It's not that bad." Cory wiggled his ankle and it hurt. "Sprained my ankle. Looks like I'm gonna be out for a week or so and it stinks. I don't fit in here and I'm worried about not practicing, you know?"

"Hey, you're a Westsider. You hold your head high!" Liam was all fired up. "Sprained ankle is nothing. Happens all the time. HBS is about football, bud. Football, that's you and me. We are *players*. That's why they come get us from the Westside. We're tough as shoe leather. We rock."

Cory laughed at his friend's enthusiasm. "I like it, Liam. See? This is why I wanted to talk to you. You sound great. So, the knee is going good, huh?"

"Uhh, let's talk about you."

"Why? Is something wrong?"

Liam paused, then explained, "Well, I got a tube pumping puss out of this thing and I need morphine to keep me from screaming out loud, so, yeah, I'd say it's all wrong."

"Sorry."

"No, that's okay. I'm gonna be fine. I'm telling you, I'll be at HBS in two short years and in the meantime, you set the tone, okay? Don't take any bull from anyone. Act like you belong, cuz you do. You deserve to be there. Got it?"

"Yeah. I got it. Thanks, Liam." Cory looked at the clock. "Hey, I gotta go, buddy. I only have so many minutes on this thing."

They said good-bye. Cory turned out the light and lay back down.

It was still dark and he still felt alone, but now there was a spark in his mind that—even though it didn't keep him warm—provided some comfort against the coming day.

Despite Liam's words, Cory still couldn't shake the feeling that he didn't fit in at HBS. He was a round peg in a square hole. Even around his new friends—Gant, Parker, and Garrison, even Jimbo—he felt out of place. Mike Chester had either gotten the message from Cheyenne or lost interest now that he had his starting job back, because he left Cory alone. Coach P was focused on getting his guys ready for the opening game, and he ignored Cory since he wasn't part of the drills.

"Just watch and try to learn as much as you can," were the only words Coach P had for Cory. He felt useless standing off to the side of the action, watching and waiting for five thirty to roll around. That's when everyone had agreed that Mr. Muiller would pick Cory up and take him to treatment up at the university.

The highlight of his week was when Cheyenne put her

hand on his arm during their Wednesday car ride to school. She looked at him with those amazing blue eyes that burned in the frame of her blond mane, her red blouse open at the collar. "Don't worry, you don't ever have to sing. No one will bother you."

Cory didn't bother to tell her that singing had dropped way down on his list of concerns. All he wanted now was to get back into the action and become the Touchdown Kid once more.

The lowlight was Thursday morning when he saw Cheyenne talking to an eighth-grade boy in the hallway between classes. She stood leaning against the lockers, holding her books tight, her blue-painted toes wiggling in her sandals. When Cory walked by, she didn't even look his way.

Otherwise, Cory slogged along, learning his school lessons, going to study hall, standing on the sideline watching practice, and heading up to SU to get treatments from Zach Houlaires before dinner with his new family. The cut on his hand healed quickly and he finished *The Outsiders,* a total bore, then rewarded himself with a John Grisham legal thriller from the school library about a boy trapped in an old hotel with his crazy father.

By the weekend, Cory's ankle felt much better. Mr. Muiller took Cory to see the trainer before Saturday's practice. Cory walked into the college facility with barely a limp. Zach came out of his office at the sight of Mr. Muiller. This time, the tables around the training room were filled with men, college players nursing bad elbows, knees, necks, shoulders, and ankles. Zach had a table set aside for Cory, though, and he connected a compression boot before slipping it on Cory's lower leg.

The players around the room eyed Cory with curiosity, but Zach and Mr. Muiller ignored them. After the compression boot, some electric stimulation, and a session with the ultrasound wand, Zach sat at the end of the table on a stool and tested Cory's ankle, probing with his fingers and then bending it around. It wasn't comfortable, but it didn't hurt enough to make Cory flinch either.

Zach frowned in a way that made Cory nervous before he announced, "I'd keep him out of practice today and ice this tonight and tomorrow, but Monday, he'll be good to go."

"Zach, I appreciate this." Mr. Muiller shook hands with the trainer. "You're the best."

"Let's have him wear this brace." Zach removed a black ankle brace from beneath the table and handed it to Cory. "Make sure it's snug when you put it on."

Cory took the brace and blinked. "I can practice?"

"Good to go on Monday." Zach stood up and dusted his hands. "Yes."

As much as Cory loved football, he had never been so excited to dive back into practice. He shook the trainer's hand and grinned the whole ride to the school, thankful that this was one of the last times he'd have to stand there like a post. Cory listened to Mr. Muiller talk on his cell phone to a banker about an apartment complex that he intended to buy. The inside of the car was soft and smelled of new leather.

Cory wondered what it would be like, having important people like Zach do you favors and then buying and selling the homes where thousands of people lived with just a phone call. Maybe he'd buy apartment complexes too one day. If he made it to the NFL, he'd have to buy something with all that money. First, though, he'd get his mom a house, something like the Muillers', with a pool and a maid like Helga and a Range Rover in the garage, maybe a white one so it wouldn't be exactly like Mrs. Muiller's.

Cory's dream was interrupted by a poke in his shoulder. "Huh?"

"I said, 'I bet you can't wait till Monday, right?'"

"I can't. I was just thinking that." Cory beamed.

"That'll put a stopper in some of these people." Mr. Muiller frowned.

"People?" Cory asked as the school came into sight.

"Every exceptional man has his doubters." Mr. Muiller steered his big Bentley sedan around to the back of the school. "There's a saying that you measure the greatness of a man by the strength of his enemies."

Cory said, "What enemies?"

Cory didn't realize anyone but Mike Chester felt that strongly about him.

"Well, it's just a saying. A lot of eyes on you and Gant. A lot of resources." Mr. Muiller braked the car and looked at the back entrance. "Jimbo's already here. His mom texted me. Go on in. We'll pick you guys up, and then your mom's coming for a visit this afternoon, right?"

"Yes." Relief and joy bloomed in Cory's heart. A number of times that week, late at night in the loneliness of his bedroom, he'd considered calling her, but he'd stayed strong, telling himself that he'd see her soon and there was no sense in worrying her. He had to be a man. "Thank you, Mr. Muiller. For taking me to Zach and getting this thing better. Thank you for everything."

"Don't worry. You'll pay me back plenty when you run for

touchdowns and catch some passes from Jimbo." Mr. Muiller clapped Cory on the shoulder.

"I will," Cory said as he slipped out of the car and headed straight for the field, smiling and excited.

When Coach P saw Cory, he asked, "Well? You good to go today?"

That deflated Cory. "Uh, they said Monday."

"Hmm." Coach P turned his back and walked away, leaving Cory to stand on the sideline again, out of the action, and apparently out of Coach P's thoughts.

Practice was like watching ice melt.

Cory stood there, burning up. He even considered going into the locker room, getting into his gear, and just practicing anyway. That would make a statement to Coach P about how badly he wanted to play, but it might make Mr. Muiller mad, especially if he reinjured his ankle and had to start all over again. So, he gritted his teeth and watched and tried to learn the plays.

During a water break, Gant and Parker and Garrison came over to him to say hello, but that and a couple of limp fist bumps was all they had time for before Coach P blew his whistle and started practice back up again.

Every so often the battle cry of the varsity team on the next field distracted him. Cory told himself he'd be there one day, and missing a week of sixth-grade football would seem like a million miles away.

After practice, he didn't even go into the locker room but found Mrs. Muiller's Range Rover in the line of parents picking up kids. Jimbo dragged himself out of the school and slumped down in the front seat, the picture of misery.

"Tuckered out, Jimbo?" chirped his mom.

"Brutal."

"Well, a dip in the pool will revive you," she said.

Jimbo swung around and eyed Cory. "How much longer are you on vacation?"

Cory clenched his hands and buried them under his legs. "The trainer said I can practice Monday."

"Great." Jimbo sounded like he thought it was anything but great.

"He's gonna be your star runner," sang Jimbo's mom.

"I don't know about that." Jimbo yawned. "Mike Chester's been tearing it up."

"Oh." Jimbo's mom pushed the wide sunglasses up on her face and flipped on the radio.

Cory didn't think that was true. Mike had scored a couple of touchdowns in practice over the last few days, but none today, and while he could sometimes break tackles by the smaller players, guys like Gant ate him for a snack. Mike went down easy in Cory's mind, but he held his tongue. He didn't need to argue with Jimbo. He'd show them all what he could do on Monday, and now he started to get excited about seeing his mom.

When they pulled in through the gates, he saw her tiny green car hunched off to the side of the circular driveway. Cory started to open the door before Mrs. Muiller had even stopped the SUV. "Hey now," she barked at him, but he dashed up the front steps, flung open the door, and flew through the house, knowing the Muillers took their guests straight to the back terrace overlooking the pool area.

He saw his mom from behind through the glass door. Mr. Muiller was raising a fancy beer bottle in the air and laughing at something she had said.

Cory bolted through the door.

When he saw Liam sitting there in a wheelchair, he nearly fell over.

"Liam! Mom!" Cory hugged his mom tight and reached out for a fist bump from Liam.

She held him and squeezed her grip before letting him go. "Let me look at you."

Cory was embarrassed, and he wondered how much she knew about his first week at HBS.

"Oh, you look fine, Cory." She smoothed out the wrinkles he'd left in her black sleeveless sweater. "Just fine. I don't know what I thought you would look like; you look fine."

"It's great to see you—and Liam too." Cory turned to his friend. "Look at you, in that chair. I'm surprised your mom let you come, and your brother."

Liam grinned. "Finn's got the sense God gave a fireplug. I asked my mom to call your mom. She's cool with you."

Liam looked around and sighed. "Miss this, though. The gravy train."

"One day, maybe. We've got plenty of room." Mr. Muiller raised his bottle. "You never know, Liam. Things happen."

"Yeah, they do." Liam's eyes fell on his damaged leg. "And I *will* be back. I'll be out of this chair in no time."

An uncomfortable silence fell over them. The pool filter gurgled until Cory's mom turned to Mr. Muiller. "You and Deb are so kind."

Liam whispered, "Long as you can run for touchdowns."

Cory's mom frowned, looked like she was going to say something, and then sucked on her lower lip.

Mr. Muiller cleared his throat and excused himself. "I'll get some burgers on that grill for you boys. There'll be more on the way if I know Jimbo. Probably asked the whole team over, and it's a good day for the pool."

They watched him go inside before Cory asked, "Why'd you say that?"

"What?" Liam glared at him.

"About liking you as long as you can score touchdowns."

"It's true, isn't it?" Liam angled his head toward the house. "That's what it's about."

"It's about an education, Liam." Cory's mom spoke gently.

"To you and Cory it might be." Liam snorted. "Not to them. Not to me. I'm not gonna be a lawyer."

"You don't want to get on their bad side, Liam." Cory lowered his voice. He thought about their plan for Liam to get one of the scholarships HBS offered going into ninth grade. "Not if you're gonna come back."

"Do you not want to be here now, Liam?" Cory's mom asked softly. "Is it too hard? I told you it might be."

Liam laughed and waved a hand. "Naw, I'm good. Just sayin' is all. Cory knows what I mean."

Cory thought about how painful the past week had been and what Gant had said. "Yes, I do."

"Guys like me and Cory, we've gotta be superstars on the field to fit into a place like this." Liam waved his hand around.

Cory wanted to change the subject. "You know, I almost called you this week, Mom."

"You should have. Cory, I told you, any time."

"Yeah, it was a tough week. I got hurt."

Her eyes widened with alarm; no one had told her. "Are you okay?"

"Yeah, it was my ankle. Just a sprain, but it made things . . ." Cory was going to say "tough," but given Liam's condition, that didn't sound right. "You know, everything's new. New kids. Teachers. Coaches. And everyone here knows each other already. So, just a little lonely."

"Then why didn't you call?" his mom asked.

He shrugged, wishing he hadn't gone down this path. "I'm not a baby, Mom."

"Hey." Liam came to the rescue. "How 'bout those Saints curtains in your bedroom? You gotta be loving that. Haha."

Cory rolled his eyes. "Right division, wrong team. I figured you're color-blind and just didn't know gold from red."

"No, I got the right team. The 2009 Super Bowl champions, remember?"

177

"I was too young to really remember. So were you, if you're being honest!" Cory said.

Liam was laughing now, that familiar sound, funny enough in itself to make Cory and his mom join in. The sound of the three of them like that made Cory feel even more lonely. It was like old times, but he felt certain that it couldn't last.

Mr. Muiller came outside with a platter piled high with raw burgers. "All right, here we go."

Cory's mom left her spot behind Liam's chair. "How can I help here?"

"You can let Helga make you a drink while you sit and relax. You're our guest." Mr. Muiller pointed a long spatula at the table beneath the enormous green umbrella. Turning away, he flipped the hamburger patties onto the grill.

Cory felt a spark of pride. Mr. Muiller treated his mom like she was still as important as she'd been two weeks ago. Maybe he'd been wrong in worrying so much about things not working out. Maybe Coach McMahan's assessment of him would carry him through sixth-grade football no matter what happened with injuries or coaching or locker room antics.

"I'd love a lemonade," Cory's mom said. Liam wheeled

alongside her at the table. "Liam? Cory?"

"I was thinking of Helga mixing you something stronger, Ashley," Mr. Muiller said, "but there are cans of lemonade and sodas for the boys in the cooler."

"I'll get them." Cory dug two grape Fantas and a lemonade out of the ice. He sat down with Liam and his mom, cracking open the cans. She wanted to hear about everything—his teachers, his classes, his teammates. Cory told her a nice story, keeping everything upbeat. He was grateful when Gant and Parker appeared with Jimbo, making things seem as normal as Cory had described them.

"Hey, bro." Gant bumped fists with Cory before doing the same with Liam. "Hey." Nodding at Liam's knee, he asked, "How you doin'?"

"I'm doin'." Liam sipped his soda. "They already said at the hospital they can see I'm a fast healer. I'll be outta this chair in no time."

"Look." Gant held out his hand, where two jumping beans wriggled and squirmed. "Mexican jumping beans. I won them at the fair. I had three, but . . ."

"That second one lived?" Cory asked.

Gant smiled that big smile. "I told you. It was just sleepin'. Now it's back."

Gant turned to Cory's mom. "He said we were like these beans."

"What?" Cory's mom chuckled. She wore a puzzled look. "Why?"

"Valuable property," Cory blurted out, not wanting his mom to hear anything depressing about being trapped and desperately squirming. "Those beans are a hit, right, Gant? Like us. How about a burger, Gant?"

That worked.

Gant pocketed the beans and sniffed the air. "There's burgers, and then there's *burgers*, and I smell *burgers*."

They watched Gant cross the terrace and pick up a plate before standing patiently beside Mr. Muiller in a wreath of smoke to watch the food cook.

More kids from the team soon showed up. Although only Parker, Garrison, and Gant were super friendly to Cory and Liam, the others were at least cordial. Everyone was polite to Cory's mom. He wondered how Mike Chester would have acted, but he didn't show. It was as if a spell had been lifted.

Mr. Muiller worked away at his grill with Helga doing cleanup as the team scarfed down burger after thick burger buried in cheese and ketchup. The laughter and shouts of nearly two dozen boys in a pool filled the afternoon as Cory and Liam traded chat and insults and his mom soaked up the sunshine in a lounge chair.

Liam wheeled his chair over to the edge of the terrace and then back to where Cory and his mom sat. "That's some clean pool, right?"

"Compared to Burnett Park it sure is," Cory said.

Liam laughed, then softly punched Cory's shoulder. "You can swim with your guys, you know. *I'd* swim if my knee wasn't busted."

"I know," Cory said. "But I'm fine here with you guys."

When the sun began to dip toward the treetops and their

teammates began to drift away. Cory, his mom, Liam, Jimbo, and Parker were sitting around the table when Mrs. Muiller appeared with Cheyenne and the two friends Cory had seen in their underwear. Jimbo's mom already had a lime drink in hand and she made a beeline for her husband, complaining loudly about the girls' soccer coach.

"Hi, Ms. Marco," Cheyenne said, ignoring her mother and shaking hands with Cory's mom. "These are my friends Tiffanae Litaker and Tami Lynn. The two Ts."

The girls said hello, giggled, and then headed for the grill.

"Are you going to stay for the fire, Ms. Marco?" Cheyenne asked.

"Fire?" Cory's mom raised her eyebrows.

"We have a fire pit on the other side of that hedge. It's fun when the stars come out. It's just a few of us, but you're welcome. Tami plays the guitar. Cory, you'll love it."

"Sounds more like a kids' thing," Cory's mom said, "but thank you for the offer, Cheyenne. You're as polite as your brother."

"Oh, him." Cheyenne rolled her eyes, then laughed and followed her friends.

"Cory, why are you blushing?" His mom wore a mischievous smile.

"She got him, Ms. Marco." Liam nodded at Cheyenne's long, brown legs walking away. "He fell for her. I see that. Everyone falls for her."

"You too, Liam?" Cory's mom asked. "I knew about Cory already. I was just teasing him."

"Not me, Ms. M." Liam wore an unusually serious face. "Girls are for later."

Cory opened his mouth to speak. He was going to say that it was Tiffanae and Tami he was embarrassed about, but then he'd have to explain what happened and why, and he didn't want to give that story any legs, so he kept quiet. Besides, he reasoned that every guy was awestruck by Cheyenne. It was nothing to be ashamed of.

Cory's mom looked at her watch. "Cory, are you coming home or are you staying for the fire?"

Cory hadn't known about the fire. He'd expected to go home and spend a day with his mom before returning on Sunday evening, and after the week he'd had, he hadn't thought of anything but getting home. Now, though, things didn't seem so bad, and if Cheyenne was going to be there . . .

"I know Liam has to get back, but you don't. I think you should stay." Cory's mom sounded like she was talking to a bill collector.

Cory studied her. "Really?"

She forced a smile. "I don't see why not."

"But we talked about watching a movie," Cory said, even though that discussion seemed like another lifetime.

"Cory." His mom sounded tired. "I understand if you want to be with your friends on a Saturday night."

Cory's insides tingled. He felt the pull of Cheyenne and knew how a meteorite must feel as it swerved toward the Earth. It was a free fall, thrilling and fast, but frightening, too.

As small as the decision seemed, Cory knew it was major.

Cory felt out of breath. "Nah. I'd rather see a movie with you."

The instant the words left his mouth, he wished he could reel them back in. But the grin on his mother's face could have lit a stadium, so he couldn't take them back.

Her eyes grew moist and she reached out and gave his hand a squeeze. "That is so nice."

"Well . . ." Cory looked at Liam, who nodded with something that might have been envy.

They got up and thanked their hosts.

"No fire?" Mr. Muiller asked Cory.

"I told my mom I'd see a movie with her."

"That makes sense," Mr. Muiller said to Cory before turning to Cory's mom. "Do you know what time you'll drop him off tomorrow?"

"After dinner?"

"That's fine. We may or may not be back from a visit to my folks, but if we're not here, Cory knows the alarm code, right, Cory?"

Cory remembered and wanted to snort at the simplicity of it, but he only said, "Yes. Four four four four."

Mr. Muiller walked them through the house and helped get Liam's chair down the steps and into the trunk before tying it half-shut with a piece of twine. Liam sat sideways in the back with his leg across the seat. Cory's mom tooted her horn as they pulled out of the circle and through the gates into the fading light.

"That's some place." Liam might have been talking to himself in the gloom.

Cory turned around in his seat. "You'll be there one day. You heard Mr. Muiller, they've got plenty of room."

Liam kept the faraway look in his eye and spoke dreamily. "Yeah, they do."

It was silent the rest of the drive back. Liam's mom met them at the curb of their apartment building and wheeled him off. Someone had broken the outside light above the entryway by the ramp, and the building swallowed them whole before Cory's mom headed home.

"He's going to get better, isn't he?" Cory asked his mom.

She took a breath and nodded. "You know Liam, Cory. He'll make it happen."

Cory watched the dilapidated neighborhood go by as they drove. The little car rattled and banged over the broken pavement the city hadn't fixed from the previous winter. "Bad things happen, Mom."

His mom pulled over and stopped the car to stare at him. "Why would you say that? This whole HBS thing was your dream, and it came true."

"Just . . ." Cory had so much built up inside him nothing could come out. "Forget it. It just seems like life is full of potholes, even when it looks smooth up ahead."

His mom pulled him close and kissed the top of his head. "It's not easy. Usually, it never is, Cory. But we've got each other. Even if we don't see each other every day."

Cory sighed and she drove them home.

Cory checked the street for any sign of Dirty's banged-up orange car. He had no reason to think those boys would be around, but self-preservation took over. He scanned the street. There were plenty of vehicles but no orange compacts. Cory breathed a sigh of relief and hustled out of the car. The comfortable sounds of arguing neighbors and the steady thump from the bass speaker of a party down the street filled the warm air. Still, he kept looking behind them as he followed his mom toward the porch.

Halfway there, his mom pulled up short.

Cory bumped into her and yelped.

His mom gasped. Cory's insides squirmed like snakes. He peeked around her.

Standing in the dark doorway was the shape of a large man bent over the lock.

"What are you *doing*?" Cory's mom sounded more angry than scared.

The man jumped and fumbled with something in his hands Cory couldn't see.

"Ashley? I uh . . ." The man threw his hands up in surrender. "I think I dropped my reading glasses. Maybe on the couch when I programmed the remote? You weren't home and I . . ."

He held out a hand to show her a driver's license he'd been wedging into the door lock to jimmy it open. "Sorry."

"Ohhh!" Cory's mom clenched her hands and her arms shook before she took a calming breath. "Cory, this is Marvin. Marvin, Cory."

Marvin stepped off the stoop into the dim light from the street lamp. He was well over six feet tall with short dark hair and the build of a weight lifter. He had big round cheeks and a broken smile as he extended a hand to shake. "I've heard a lot of good things about you, Cory."

Cory shook the man's hand but looked at his mom.

"Marvin's a teacher, Cory. High school biology." His mom spoke like that explained everything, but it didn't.

Cory had a million questions. How had they met? Why was he in their house programming the remote? Was he her *boyfriend*?

Cory knew by the way his mom was behaving and the way this big mope was acting that he *was* her boyfriend. She'd never had a serious boyfriend before. Cory knew it wasn't because people hadn't asked her. He'd even overheard her once tell a man from her work on the phone that she was a mother right now and didn't have time for anything else.

Now, apparently, she did have time for something else.

Time for Marvin.

"Take me back." The words leaped from Cory's mouth like men jumping from a burning building.

"Cory? What?" His mom forced a laugh.

"I want to go home," he said.

"Cory, this is your home." His mother choked on her words.

Oh, she made it easy for him, as easy as breathing. "No, it's not. It's your home. You and Marvin."

"Oh, boy." Marvin's shoulders slumped. "Ashley, I'm so sorry. I'm trying to finish up that online course and I couldn't see the screen. I was . . . getting a headache. My glasses . . ."

"You knew I wanted to talk to Cory alone, before he met you!" His mom was shaken.

Cory was already walking toward the car.

189

Cory needed something to think about as the city flashed past and his mother sniffled next to him. She had tried to talk him out of it, but after fifteen minutes of him holding firm in the front seat, she'd finally started the motor and backed out into the street. Marvin had been long gone.

Cory had the window open. He flattened his hand and let it move up and down in the rush of warm air as he thought about Cheyenne. That seemed the best antidote to his mother's tears, and it worked. He pictured that smile and the mane of blond hair and those long, tan legs. He wondered if she'd put her arm around him if he sat beside her at the fire. Just the thought of that sent shivers up his spine, and he really couldn't think about his mom. She clearly had her own life now—Marvin—and, even though a small voice inside his head told him he wasn't being reasonable or kind, he was too far down the road. All he had to do was remember the way that big mope Marvin looked at his mom.

They got off the highway and Cory's mom pulled the car into a gas station. She stopped under the cone of blue-white light. "Cory, you can't not talk to me."

He sighed. "Mom, let it go. I'm fine and so are you. I'm not a kid anymore. You've got your life and I've got mine."

He sounded way more grown-up and confident than he felt. He wasn't entirely sure he had anything at HBS yet. So far, it was all talk. He hadn't taken a snap. He was no closer to being a football star and having his own independent life than Gant's jumping beans.

"Marvin is a good man." His mom sounded desperate. She kept holding on to the wheel. "He's been coming into the store for over a year and asking me out and I always said no because we were always busy."

"Yeah, dragged down by a kid. I get it, Mom." The words came out nastier than Cory expected.

Out in front of the Quik Mart, two men argued loudly about cigarettes.

"I . . . I don't like being alone, Cory. I'm not used to it. Not all the time," she said. "It was empty without you. So, we watched TV and had tacos one night."

"I love tacos."

"Cory, I didn't want this whole HBS thing." His mother spoke softly, but now beneath the words was something hard and sharp.

Cory made an O with his hand and looked at the moon through it. "Just take me back. I don't want to miss the fire pit."

She reached out and touched his cheek with the backs of her fingers. "I love you, Cory."

"Yeah," he said, shifting his pretend telescope to the sign above the pump offering a thirty-two-ounce slushy for just ninety-nine cents. "Me too."

It wasn't much, but it was enough for her to start the car and buzz away.

When they pulled into the Muillers' circle, she leaned over and kissed his cheek. "Can I have a hug?"

"Sure, Mom." He gave her a one-armed squeeze, pulling away when she held on too tight. To distract her, he said, "We've got a scrimmage next Saturday on the varsity field at ten."

"I'll be there," she said. "Maybe we'll have lunch afterward? And if you don't have anything to do, could we take a rain check on the movie? They got *Presumed Innocent* for me. It's old, but I know you'll love it."

"Maybe, Mom." Cory got out and looked down at her through the open window.

The look on her face nearly broke him down. She was beautiful and sad and only a few weeks ago she was everything to him. He wondered if that was what it meant to grow up.

"Probably," he said.

Her smile lit up the inside of the car. She nodded. "Good. Great. 'Probably.' I like that."

Cory paused. "Are you going to see Marvin this week?"

She hesitated, then said, "Yes. He's my friend."

Cory shrugged. He knew it shouldn't hurt him, but it did, and that somehow made him ashamed. He couldn't think of anything to say, so he turned to go, expecting her to call him back.

He felt more numb with each step he took because he needed her to be the one to speak, to call him back and sort it all out. When he reached the front door, he opened it and waited half a second before closing it behind him. He stood still, hoping and waiting. Through the thick wood, he heard her car wind up and zip away.

The house was mostly dark. He passed a TV room where the backs of Mr. and Mrs. Muiller's heads tilted together above the edge of a couch as they watched an old black-and-white movie. Out back on the terrace, Cory smelled the smoke and heard the low hum of voices amid the crackle of burning wood. Beyond the pool a dark shape tossed a log into the fire pit, sending a fountain of sparks up into the trees. Jimbo's laughter rang out from the fire.

Lights glowed along the walkway. Cory made his way around the pool and through an arch of vines out to the lawn in a clearing of tall trees. More than a dozen kids sat on the circle of benches around the fire. He could pick out the enormous shape of Gant, holding a marshmallow on a stick that trembled over the flames. As his eyes adjusted, he saw the back of Cheyenne's long mane. A boy with a hoodie sat dangerously close to her and even leaned so their shoulders were touching. It was probably Mike, but Cory didn't care.

He hesitated, then touched Cheyenne's shoulder.

When he did, both she and the boy spun around.

53

Mike jumped to his feet.

"Cory? Hi!" Cheyenne got up too and swept some hair from her face before breaking out in a big white smile.

Gant looked over from his place by the fire, saw Mike and Cory, and offered a worried look.

Cory's stomach flipped. A charge of fear flew through his body. He expected Mike to drop into a martial arts stance.

Instead he flipped off his hood. "Hey, Cory. How you doing?"

Cory blinked. "I . . . uh . . ."

"Want a marshmallow stick? I was just going to roast one up. Happy to get you one, too."

"I'll take a marshmallow," Cheyenne said.

"Uh, sure," said Cory.

"Great." Mike bounded off into the trees.

Cheyenne watched him go.

Cory said, "For real?"

Cheyenne laughed. "He's not so bad, right?"

"I have no idea," Cory said.

"People can change, Cory." She glanced at the spot where Mike had gone. "I explained to him how it had to be, and he promised he'd be good. Funny that you showed up, though. Good for him. I didn't know if he could really do it."

Cory looked over at the spot where Mike had disappeared and now popped back into view holding up two long sticks like a victorious warrior. "Got 'em!"

Chester bounded back and handed Cory a stick before turning toward the fire. "Parker, you got the marshmallow bag? C'mon, buddy. Save some for Cory and me. Haha."

Cory had a hard time processing it all. Was Mike actually handing him a marshmallow?

"Uh, thanks." Cory took it and poked it through with the narrow end of his stick, then remembered his own manners and turned to Cheyenne. "Can I make you one?"

She laughed. "Well, I think he's making me one, but I ran a lot today, so why not have two? Sure, Cory. Thanks."

Cory felt as silly as a duck on ice.

He put two marshmallows on his stick, watching Mike from the corner of his eye as the stick wavered over the orange flames. Cory hadn't roasted marshmallows before, so he tried to rotate them around the way Mike was doing. Jimbo popped a roasted marshmallow of his own into his mouth, chewed, and watched Cory with a curious expression. When Mike's began to smoke and turn golden brown, Cory thrust his own too near the coals and they burst into flames.

Jimbo's laugh was muffled by a mouthful of melted marshmallow.

Parker stepped up from his seat on a bench, took the flaming stick from Cory, and blew the burning candy out like a birthday candle. "Gotta start over. You got too close to the heat."

"Here, Cory. Have mine. I can do another." Mike Chester pushed a golden marshmallow off the stick and into Cory's hand before Cory could say a word. Without pausing, Mike turned to Cheyenne and gave her the other one. Then he dug two more out of the bag, skewered them, and began to roast.

Cheyenne beamed up at Mike before turning to Cory. "Have it, Cory. It's good. Like this." She popped the whole thing into her mouth and chewed, smiling.

Cory did the same, and the warm, sweet candy exploded through its crispy brown skin, filling his mouth with a hint of smoke that only made the marshmallow more delicious. "Wow."

Gant had disappeared, but now he was back with two cans of Sprite. "Want one?"

"Sure." Cory cracked the can and sat down on the other side of Cheyenne, leaving Mike's spot alone in a gesture of peace. Gant sat on Cory's other side and sipped his own soda. The flames flickered in Gant's dark eyes as he stared.

"Some life, huh?" Gant spoke low so that only Cory could hear him. "Being rich like these kids?"

Cory leaned toward Gant and kept his voice even lower. "Do you think this whole thing with Mike Chester is for real?"

Jimbo threw another log on the fire. Everyone gasped or laughed as a thousand orange dots of light swam toward the sky.

Cheyenne's voice rang out pleasantly. "Careful, Jimbo!"

Gant turned his dark, glittering eyes on Cory. "Mike being nice is as real as that cloud of sparks, bro."

Cory looked back at the peaceful glow of the fire. "What sparks?"

Gant said, "Exactly."

Cory sat around the fire until the last person had gone home. He could barely keep his eyes open as Cheyenne touched his arm and said good night, but once in bed, he had a hard time falling asleep. He thought about calling his mom, but cringed at the thought that Marvin might be there. If he was, Cory didn't want to know about it. Instead, he dialed Liam, knowing that the only phone in his house was in the kitchen, which was right across the hall from Liam's bedroom.

It rang three times and Cory was about to hang up when a rough voice answered the phone.

"Yeah?"

Cory gulped at the sound of Finn's voice, but a jolt of panic and fear wouldn't allow him to hang up. "Uh . . . it's Cory. Is Liam there?"

"Yeah."

Cory heard rustling and a double *thunk* as the phone bounced off the floor, then a distant voice. "Hey, fathead. It's your girlfriend."

More rustling could be heard before Liam got on. "Hey, Cory! That was fun today. I am so pumped up to get well. I really think Mr. Muiller would have us both live there, don't you? He seemed like he liked the idea."

"Yeah, I do." Cory felt himself being washed away in Liam's excitement. "There's another room right next to mine and you could have this one with all this Saints garbage."

"Garbage?" Liam faked shock.

They both laughed.

"They are so rich, right?" Liam said. "You think Mr. Muiller inherited it, or you think he made it himself?"

"Himself," Cory said, proud of his patron and thinking of the conversation he'd overheard about buying up apartment buildings. "The guy is super smart."

"Except for his security code, right?" Liam laughed. "I mean, how smart is that? Four four four four? Four fours! It's their doggone *street address*. C'mon, a circus monkey could come up with a better code."

Cory lowered his voice. "Maybe Mrs. Muiller came up with it."

Liam made chimp noises. "Oo-oo-oo-oo! Four four four four! Oo-oo! I got four thousand four hundred and forty-four diamonds, too. Oo-oo-oo!"

They both burst out laughing again.

A witchlike shriek in the background cut them off. "Liam! Get off that phone! You're supposed to be sleepin'!"

"Gotta go, Cory. I'll talk to you soon." Liam clunked down the phone, leaving Cory in dark silence.

Cory chuckled to himself and snapped shut his phone with a sigh. He wondered how Liam could have such a great attitude living with two monsters. It made Cory feel lucky, and he decided the next time he saw Marvin he wasn't going to be so mean.

It rained all day Sunday. Cory did some homework, read his book, and played a little Xbox with Jimbo in the game room, but most of the time they were planted alongside Mr. Muiller, watching NFL games on the big screen. Cheyenne was out with friends. Maybe it was the gloomy day or the poor night of sleep or Cheyenne being gone, but Cory felt a nagging loneliness all day, even though he wasn't alone. He kept thinking about the last rainy day with his mom. It had felt so nice, just the two of them watching movies from the couch, her hand scratching his head from time to time. The patter against the windows and roof were a comfort on that day. Now, it just felt wet.

The next day in school, the spark of friendship between Mike and Cory continued to glow. When Cory rounded a corner in the hallway before science class and saw Cheyenne and Mike leaning up against the same locker together, talking and smiling, he knew exactly what was happening.

"It's a rope-a-dope, Gant," Cory told his friend. "Don't *stare*."

"It's not against the law to look," Gant said. "Cor, she's a nuclear bomb."

"Just stay cool." Cory nudged his giant friend to the other side of the hallway so the two of them could pass with plenty of traffic in between them and Cheyenne.

"Hey, Cory! Gant!" Mike had spotted them and he waved. "What's up, guys?"

"Just science class," Cory said, putting on a smile. "Hey, Cheyenne."

"Hey, Cory. Hey, Gant. What's up, boys?"

Cory swallowed and silently urged Gant to keep going.

Gant leaned down as they went. "What's a rope-a-dope?"

"Muhammad Ali? That rope-a-dope?" Cory saw nothing in Gant's eyes.

"You gotta watch some History Channel, Gant."

Gant shrugged. They entered their science class and sat down.

"When Ali fought George Foreman for the title," Cory said. "He came out and just let Foreman pound him. He kept his back to the rope and covered up. He let Foreman go wild, throwing punch after punch after punch."

"So, Mike Chester is letting you punch his lights out? That's what you're saying? I don't get that," Gant said.

"No, no." Cory shook his head. "After Foreman was dog-tired from throwing all those punches, which weren't really hurting Ali, Ali came out and destroyed Foreman. Mike is taking punches right now like he's on the ropes and ready to go down, but he's not. I don't trust him."

"Hey, the guy roasted you a marshmallow. That was sweet." Gant laughed, then got serious as their teacher strolled in.

"Yeah, well let's see how things go at practice," Cory said, "when he has to start splitting reps with me. Maybe Coach P even puts me on the first team?"

"He is?" Gant wrinkled his brow.

"I don't know. You never know. I'm trying. I'm Coach McMahan's guy, right?" Cory sat up straight. "I'm gonna float like a butterfly and sting like a bee."

"I don't think it's gonna work that way, but you never know," Gant said.

The bell rang and their science teacher picked up his marker and began to write on the board.

Cory opened his notebook and picked up a pen. "You know what else Ali said? He said, 'Impossible is not a fact. It's an opinion.'"

Cory heard the howling as he pushed open the locker room door.

"Ohhhh! Ohhhh! The Ravens stink. The Ravens stink." Garrison Green sounded like he was in pain. On his face, like a gas mask, was a jockstrap. He marched around the locker room, groaning and barking out his allegiance to the Patriots as the rest of the team laughed their heads off.

"What's that about?" Cory asked Gant.

Gant snorted and rumbled with delight. "Every time the Patriots play the Ravens, Garrison and Parker bet a walk of shame. Whoever's team loses has to wear a jock on his face, groan like he's dyin', and say his team stinks—and he's gotta call them out by name—a dozen times."

Cory laughed but then cut it short and opened his locker. The whole thing about guys making fools of themselves reminded him of singing and swirlies, and that was something he wanted to forget, even if Mike was being nice to him now.

Cory slipped the pads out of his locker and onto his frame. They felt awkward and tight after a week off, but he wasn't about to complain. He needed to perform. Pushing the discomfort from his mind, he joined up with Gant and Garrison marching toward the field. The sound of the varsity's crunching feet approached from behind like a storm. The sixth-graders stepped aside and watched them snake down the hill and out onto their field.

Gant was awestruck. "They went down to New Jersey Friday night and beat Don Bosco by two touchdowns."

"Yeah, I heard they won," Cory said. "Mr. Muiller was pretty pumped up, but who's Don Bosco?"

"You mean *what* is Don Bosco."

"Okay. What is Don Bosco?"

Gant stared. "You're kiddin', right?"

"Gant, give me a break."

"Don Bosco is one of the top twenty high school football teams in the country," Gant said. "In New Jersey? No? You got a lot to learn, bro. You're in the big time, now."

"Let's go."

Cory worked the kinks out of his body. Agility drills left him gassed. The smell of baking grass made him queasy. Sweat trickled down the valley of his back beneath the shoulder pads. Either the grass or the dust made him itch, too. He burst from one individual-period drill to the next, making sure to be first. He thought he saw Coach P break into a reluctant smile, but he wasn't certain. One thing he did know was that if he beat Mike to the front, Mike was politely lining up behind him. That was a relief.

Cory started feeling fast and good and he forgot about the discomfort of the pads and the heat.

When they got to the cut drill, Coach P whipped out his watch. "Okay, Mr. Touchdown Kid. I got times on all these other cupcakes, but let's see what you got now that you're playing on two good wheels. No excuses, right?"

"No, sir." Cory scanned the cones and went over in his mind the pattern he'd make through the drill. He wanted to plant his foot just outside the cone, minimizing the distance he had to go.

"Ready?" Coach P held up his stopwatch. "On your movement."

Cory crouched into a stance and burst forward. He felt a bit sloppy in his turns but fast in the straightaways, and he leaned forward as he crossed the finish line.

Coach P snorted and held the watch up where Cory couldn't see it. "Hey, Jimbo. Take a look at your adopted brother's time."

57

Cory watched Jimbo squint through his face mask but couldn't read his face.

Cory circled the coach and stretched his neck. Coach P didn't try to hide the watch from him, but before Cory could react, Jimbo said, "Wow."

"Yeah, wow." Coach P turned the watch face toward himself as if he wasn't quite sure he'd been correct. He gave a short nod, then pushed the watch at Cory.

It read 9.3.

"You just might be a running back, son." Coach P gave Cory a smile before he pocketed the watch and tooted his whistle. "Okay, you cupcakes, let's get it going. Let me see some business."

Cory beamed and looked down to hide his smile. He ran through the cut drill two more times and wished Coach P had put a watch on them too, because he felt even faster. He had a new spring in his step, a new confidence, and it didn't hurt that no one was harassing him about singing or shooting him dirty glances or fighting him for a spot in line. He gulped water at the horse during a break, and when he straightened up, there was Mike Chester.

"Nice time," Mike said.

Cory still couldn't believe this was the same kid who'd looked at him so hatefully only a week ago, but then he reminded himself of the power of Cheyenne. Even out on the football field in the midst of the sweat and the heat, the image of her made him wobbly.

"Thanks."

"When Coach calls for first team, though, I'm still going out there," Mike said without blinking. "I'm being a good teammate, but that doesn't mean I roll over."

"Uh . . ." Cory didn't know how to respond. He was totally off guard. "Okay."

"Okay, just didn't want to get in a thing about it. Thanks." Mike nodded and turned away, snapping up his chinstrap.

In a strange way, it almost felt good that his rival had said what he said to Cory.

"What was that about?" Parker jogged beside Cory as they headed for the inside run drill.

"Nothing," Cory said. "He's just saying that when Coach calls for first team, he's going to take the spot like last week. Doesn't want to fight with me."

"For real?" Parker's mouthpiece fell out of his mouth, but he snatched it before it could hit the ground. "Mike is being *polite* to you?"

"I know," Cory said. "But he is."

"Love you like a love song, baby."

"What?"

"He'd shave his head if Cheyenne said she liked bald guys."

Cory laughed, thinking he'd shave his head too.

The coach looked up from his practice sheet and blew his whistle. "Give me that first-team backfield and O-line in an I formation, on the ball!"

Cory couldn't help hoping for a miracle, that the coach would tell Mike Chester to step aside, but he didn't. Mike lined up behind Parker, who played fullback, with Jimbo in front of them both at quarterback and Gant stepping into his spot at left tackle with the rest of the line.

"Coach Tackitt, get me a defense out here!"

Before Cory could think, a flood of players took up all the spots for a 4-3 defense. It was as if he weren't there, and he ended up with the other dozen backups and a handful of scrubs lined up along the forty-yard line behind the offense, watching. He focused on Mike Chester, listening to the plays called, telling himself what to do, and matching that with what Mike did, both right and wrong. The first-team offense ran ten plays before Coach P called for the second team.

Cory bolted from his spot, heading for the huddle.

Just as he got there, a backup running back named Dante Quackmire—everyone called him Duck—arrived at the same spot. Duck was fast but much smaller than Cory. Neither of them gave any ground though. Cory couldn't believe that he wouldn't return from his injury as at least the second-team running back. He searched Coach P's face to find out.

The black dots of Coach P's eyes darted back and forth between Cory and Duck, and his tongue poked out from the corner of his mouth as though he was about to speak.

58

"Yeah, let's see Cory run it." Coach P pointed to the defense gathering like young chicks around Coach Tackitt. "Duck, you can play some scout team at free safety. You can work on your reads."

Duck's face fell so far and so hard that Cory felt bad for the boy as he slumped and shuffled off to the scout team.

Brady Swabb, the starting outside linebacker, patted Duck on the back. "C'mon, Duck. Who wants to play offense when you can be over here with the *real* hitters?"

Coach P turned his eyes back on Cory, and now they were ice cold. "I wanna see some real business out of you, Cory. I can get Duck back here real fast."

Cory felt the chill. "Okay, Coach."

Coach P turned to Parker, who looked more like an offensive guard than the backup quarterback. "Gimme a pro set, split-slot left forty-eight sweep. Let's see if this dog can hunt."

Cory trembled as Parker repeated the play and they broke the huddle. He looked over at Garrison, who stayed in with the second team because the backup fullback was nursing a pulled hamstring. "Good, right?"

"If you mean do I got the cornerback, you better believe it." Garrison's words and smile came garbled through his mouthpiece. "I'm gonna flatten that cupcake."

Cory gave a short nod like he was all in. He'd do his part too, even though half the scout team was now made up of top players. Mike was at the strong safety position, the only player on the field who'd get a clean shot at him.

Cory was determined to shine, no matter what. "Let's do this."

They got set and the ball was snapped. Cory took the toss, following Garrison toward the sideline. From the corner of his eye, Cory saw the line give way like a wet paper bag. The defense poured through. Brady Swabb, the speedy outside linebacker running low and hard, led the way.

He sprang forward.

Garrison blasted the cornerback, knocking him toward the sideline but also eliminating Cory's ability to get to the outside. Mike read the play and was closing fast at the perfect angle. Half the defensive line was in hot pursuit. There was no room for Cory to cut one way or another. The only thing to do was meet Mike at the line. It was a no-win for Cory; Mike had a free shot and ten yards of momentum, top speed. In the moment before the collision, Cory felt it all slipping away and knew what it must be like for the circus trapeze artist to fly gracefully into space, dazzling everyone, only to see the swing fly just out of reach.

The only difference between Cory and the trapeze artist was that the circus performer had a net. He'd live to try again. Cory knew he wouldn't get a second chance. It was maybe a fraction of a second, but it would alter his universe.

Cory lowered his shoulder without thinking. He ripped up under Mike's pads, exploding into him, planting a foot, and breaking to the outside where the gap between him and the cornerback was widening.

His rival flew, hands flying.

Cory darted forward, away from the herd of linemen. The cornerback reached out for him. Cory slapped his hands away like an angry mom protecting her cookie jar. He planted again and cut straight upfield.

No one could catch up to him, but Duck had an angle from his spot at free safety and he had payback on his mind. Cory feinted at him and switched the ball to his outside arm. Duck dove low, aiming for Cory's knees. Cory planted and jabbed and stabbed his free hand down into Duck's helmet, driving his face into the dirt, slipping free from his arms, and surging all the way into the end zone at top speed.

He didn't shuffle or dance or spike the ball. Cory turned with it tucked under his arm like a grocery package and jogged all the way back to the huddle. He delivered the football to Coach P and moved to his spot where the huddle could soon form around him.

No one said a word.

Cory worried that he'd done something wrong, but it was just surprise that kept them quiet until Gant recovered his senses and let go a war whoop and nearly knocked Cory over before hugging him and lifting him into the air.

"That's my bro!" Gant chortled. "Touchdown Kid! Scholarship players . . . represent!"

"Gant, put him down before you twist his other ankle!" Coach P was not amused.

Gant set Cory down, but he shook with joy in the huddle and practically danced all the way to the line of scrimmage. Cory fought back a smile, then got serious.

Parker took the snap and dropped back. Cory's job was to block the outside linebacker, protecting the quarterback on a pass play. Brady Swabb raced around the edge of the formation. Cory got low and exploded up into him. Pads cracked. Cory felt a jolt, but Brady staggered sideways before slipping an arm over Cory's pad and racing toward Parker.

Parker threw the pass downfield a second before Brady got there.

"Not bad, Marco. That's good business." Coach P looked down at his script, moving on. "I like a back that blocks."

Cory glowed with pride.

There were two more pass plays before Cory got his next chance. It was a lead play, right up the gut of the defense. On the snap, Cory tucked in behind big Garrison Green, who rumbled like a freight train through the four hole in the right side of the line. Garrison hammered the middle linebacker. Cory cut away from the block, toward the sideline, only to be blown up—literally blasted into the air.

He never saw it coming.

His legs were over his head and he crashed to the dirt, twisting his neck. A bolt of electric pain shot down his right arm.

Mike Chester stood above him, bellowing and victorious with fists raised high.

Cory lay still, not to be dramatic, but because he couldn't get up.

"What'd you do, you piece of crap!" Gant shot into the picture above Cory, wispy white clouds and a flat blue sky his backdrop.

Gant jammed his hands into Mike's torso, flicking him out of the scene like a booger. Gant gathered himself and bent over, hands on knees. "Cor, you okay?"

Coach P appeared, red faced and shouting. "Gant! Take a lap! You don't hit your teammates after the whistle!"

Gant straightened, standing as tall as his coach and rumpling his face angrily. "That was a cheap shot, Coach! We're supposed to protect our backs."

Coach P went purple. White flecks of spit flew from his mouth as he yelled, "I said a *lap*! Now get on your horse and ride!"

Gant's shoulders sank. He turned and jogged off.

Coach P knelt down beside Cory. "You okay, son? What hurts?"

Cory's numbness became a prickly tingle. "My neck. I'm okay."

Cory tried to sit up.

"Whoa, whoa." Coach P pinned him down. "You just lie still till we figure this out."

The head coach looked up but kept his hands on Cory. "Coach Tackitt, take my practice sheet. Move the drill and keep going. I got this. Let's go! Get back to business!"

Mike Chester appeared now. "Cory, you okay? I'm sorry, man . . ."

"It was a clean hit, Mike," Coach P said. "That's football. He'll be okay, right, Cory?"

Cory had no idea, but he wasn't going to argue. "Yeah. I'm good."

"Okay, 'cuz I just . . ."

"It's okay, Mike. Get back to business now. I got this." Coach P spoke with a kindness Cory didn't know he had, and Mike disappeared. Coach P had his phone out now. "Kayla? Yeah, it's me. Can I get you on the sixth-grade field? I got a neck . . . No, I'm not sure how bad."

Cory panicked, because if someone said it, it might make it true, and he tried to sit up again. "Coach, no. I'm okay. Honest."

"You just relax. Kayla will tell us if you're okay or not, not you. Not me."

Cory blinked as the sun burned through the edge of a cloud. He could smell the grass and the sour scent of Coach P's sweat, maybe his breath too. He heard his own breathing and concentrated on his hands and feet. He could feel them now. That was good. He wiggled his fingers, then his toes. Everything worked. He took a deep breath and let it out.

Soon he heard the sounds of practice and knew that football kept going—with you or without you. The choke hold of fear tightened and a gurgle escaped his throat.

"You okay?" Coach P looked concerned.

"Yeah, Coach."

Kayla Rice arrived and Cory struggled to sit up again.

"Don't move." Worry crept over her face and her voice had an edge.

Fear ate into Cory's bones.

She tested his hands, having him squeeze, verifying that he could feel her touch on the backs of his hands. She asked him where it hurt and how he felt.

"I'm okay," he said. "It hurt my neck, but I'm okay now."

"He got dumped pretty good," Coach P said.

The trainer went over him again, shining a penlight in his eyes, asking him questions about the date and the president, and finally probing his spine with her fingers before she sat him up slowly and looked at Coach P.

In the tone reserved for a funeral parlor, Coach P asked, "What do you think?"

Cory had that sick feeling that always washes in before the bad news. And he had to ask himself, "Why can't things just go right?"

Kayla Rice straightened up and held out a hand to help Cory up. "I think he'll be okay. If he's up to it, you can put him back in."

When Cory got to his feet, the trainer scolded him like he'd already done something wrong. "But if you feel anything, dizzy, shots of pain, confusion, you tell Coach and we'll get you out."

"No, I'm all right." Cory was scared that he might be seriously hurt, but he was more scared of losing everything.

Kayla's phone rang. She answered it, said she had to go, and jogged off toward the varsity field. Coach P put a hand on Cory's shoulder pad. "You good?"

"I wanna go back in, Coach. I'm fine."

Coach P nodded toward the huddle, where Duck had

slipped back into Cory's spot. "Okay. Let's see some business."

Cory tapped Duck on the back and directed him with a thumb. "Coach wants me in."

The player opened his mouth to complain, but then he saw Coach P's face and slouched off.

Cory took his spot. Gant beamed at him from across the huddle and gave him two thumbs-up. "Yeah, bro."

Coach P took his practice sheet back from Coach Tackitt, checked it, and spoke to Parker. "Let's see a spread right forty-seven veer."

Parker repeated the play and broke the huddle. Cory lined up. On the snap, Gant made a hole so big Cory wondered if the defense was playing down a man. He shot through the hole, broke back inside off the wide receiver's block, and turned on the speed. He saw Mike from the corner of his eye.

Mike launched himself at Cory's knees. It was like a rewind playback, only this time Cory launched himself up and over Mike, hurdling his rival and barely nicking his helmet with a toe. Cory kept going, gave a head fake to the free safety that left him in a heap, and then pranced into the end zone untouched.

He jogged back and tossed the ball to Coach P without comment.

"Now that's some business."

Cory bit into his mouthpiece to keep from grinning.

Gant giggled and hip-bumped him. "You're a megaton bomb, bro."

"Gant!" Coach P barked. "This ain't a dance floor! Get in the huddle."

Gant giggled his way back into the huddle, expressing the joy Cory felt but was too cautious to show—first, because he was still an outsider, and second, because he was afraid it wouldn't last.

Tuesday in school, Gant met Cory outside his English class to walk to their science class together.

"What's so funny?" Gant asked.

"Nothing," Cory said.

"Well, your smile is so big it must hurt."

"Just a writing assignment," Cory said. "Five-page argumentative essay. I love it."

Gant stopped him. "Cor, you hurt your neck, right?"

"Yeah." Cory rubbed where it was sore.

"Well, you must've hurt your head too. Your brains are scrambled. No one smiles over a five-page paper."

Cory shrugged and kept going. "It's my thing. It's what lawyers do every day—they take a side and argue for their clients."

Gant's disbelief kept him quiet until they saw Cheyenne and Mike leaning against a locker outside science class. "Oh boy," Gant muttered. "I thought she was over him."

"They're friends," Cory said with a lightness he didn't feel.

When Cheyenne saw him, however, she quickly said good-bye to Mike and walked over to Cory. "How's the neck?"

"Uh . . . good." Cory found it hard to speak.

"Good." She smiled and touched his arm before heading off to her class.

"Oh, honeybunch," Gant said in a high-pitched voice, *"how's your necky-poo?"*

Gant toyed with Cory's hair until Cory swatted his hand away. "Cut it out. She's just being nice."

"Nice?" Gant's eyebrows jumped. "Bro, she's sweet for you. You see how fast she dropped Mike? Like a hot rock."

"Nah," Cory said, but the words stuck to the inside of his brain like chewing gum, making it hard to concentrate the rest of the day.

It wasn't until he took his first hit at football practice that he remembered how sore his neck was. Cory gritted his teeth and forced himself to run just as hard, though, because Mike Chester wasn't letting up. Cory's rival had possibly the best day ever running the ball.

After being bowled over by Mike on his way into the end zone, Duck got up slowly and announced, "Hey, Mike, maybe we should call *you* the Touchdown Kid."

"Maybe we should call you Daffy Duck instead of just plain 'Duck,'" Gant growled.

"Easy, Gant," Duck muttered quietly, "I'm just sayin'."

Three plays later, it was Cory's turn. He saw stars of pain as he blasted through the line on an off-tackle play, powering over the top of Brady before zipping past Duck on his way to the end zone.

"Here you go, Duck." Cory tossed him the football on his way back to the huddle. "A souvenir for you, from the Touchdown Kid."

While no one came right out and said it, Cory knew he was in a heated competition with Mike. He only wished his neck didn't ache so badly. After dinner that night, he holed up in his room to work on his paper and ice his neck. If Cheyenne hadn't been at a friend's working on a scene from *Romeo and Juliet* for the school play, Cory would have likely stayed upstairs until bedtime. Alone in his room with a paper that proved harder than he'd thought it would and a throbbing in his neck, he began to doubt himself. For inspiration, he decided to call Liam.

"This thing is killing me, Liam." He sat on the bed with his feet up and the wet ice bag sloshing behind his neck. "It's like someone is stabbing me with a knife."

"Buddy, I wish I was in your shoes," Liam said. "Now is when you separate yourself. Being hurt is part of the game. As long as you're not injured—like *I* am—you gotta just power through it. Westside, Cory. We're hungry and we're tough. We fight . . . Westside."

"Yeah." Cory tried not to sound glum.

"Say it, Cor. 'Westside.'"

"Westside."

"Not like that, come on! *Westside!*"

"Westside!" Cory raised his voice. "Westside!"

63

Cory got through Wednesday, but he wasn't shouting "Westside," he was just trying to survive. His neck throbbed with pain through the day. When he saw Cheyenne, she was talking to that eighth-grade kid Cory sometimes saw her with, and maybe she didn't see him, but she didn't drop the eighth-grader when Cory walked by.

Practice was a grind. He tried not to let the neck affect him, but he finished the day doubting himself once again.

Cheyenne was at dinner, and it raised his spirits when she addressed him.

"So, people are talking, Cory." Cheyenne stabbed a cherry tomato with her fork and paused before eating it. "Tiffanae said her brother—he's on the varsity—said that Coach McMahan yelled at the running backs and said he's got a sixth-grader who runs harder than them. He didn't say your name, but she said everyone started talking about the Touchdown Kid . . ."

"How do you know he wasn't talking about Mike Chester?" Jimbo asked.

"Jimbo!" Jimbo's mom swatted him with her napkin.

Cheyenne frowned. "Cory's here to get *you* to be all-state, and that's what you say?"

"Well, throw me in jail." Jimbo sulked. "I'm only sayin' that Mike's been playing out of his mind all of a sudden. And anyway, you're the one who likes him."

Cheyenne sighed. "Forsooth. Deb, talk to your son, will you? Cory's his ticket—everyone says so—and he needs to be more supportive. Disloyalty is *'the most unkindest cut of all.'*"

"There she goes." Jimbo rolled his eyes.

"Cory's here so HBS has a run game that opens up the pass for you to do your thing, Jimbo," Mr. Muiller rumbled.

"See?" Cheyenne made a face.

"Wait, I'm not finished." Mr. Muiller held up his hand. "Sometimes competition brings out the best in people, and football is all about competition."

Cory knew what that meant, and it didn't make him feel any better.

Cory was sore and exhausted on Thursday after ladder runs when Coach P dismissed the team and called for him and Mike to remain.

"Take a seat, men." Coach P motioned them toward the bench and kept talking in low tones with his two assistant coaches. Cory and Mike exchanged an anxious glance as he turned to them.

Cory had scored an impressive seven touchdowns during practice; Mike only had three. The air had been filled with cheers of "Touchdown Kid," and they hadn't been for Mike. So Cory was feeling pretty good when Coach P drilled his small dark eyes into the two of them. "Okay, men, here's how it goes. You both look good. Chester, you've got more experience in the offense and you're built tough. Marco, you've got more speed and natural talent, but you're not as durable."

Cory opened his mouth to protest. He'd been playing with an aching neck all week and lighting it up, but Coach P wasn't asking for comments.

"So, Saturday we got a live scrimmage against B'ville, and I'm splitting your reps with the first team. I'll let the numbers decide who the starter is going to be for our games. It's all about the numbers. That makes it simple and fair. Good luck to both of you. That's all." Coach P turned and walked away.

Cory sat, stunned for a moment, before he realized Mike was holding out a hand for Cory to shake.

He said, "Good luck," sounding like he meant it.

"Thanks." Cory shook his hand. "You too."

Mike got up and jogged away. Cory sat looking around at the private-school fields with their thick grass and a sweeping view of nearby wooded hills. It was so far from his battered old Westside neighborhood, haunted by Dirty and Hoagie and now that fathead Marvin. It was a world he wanted to stay in, this soft, green place where bleachers were built with fresh-pressed aluminum. He ran his fingers along the grooves in the bench. No graffiti. No scratches or stains. It was a clean, strong place meant for minting football superstars.

Cory sighed and headed for the locker room. He told Gant the deal and Gant whispered that the job was as good as his.

He joined Jimbo—who had treated him great after the discussion at dinner and now that he was playing like a champion. They got in the Range Rover, chatting while Mrs. Muiller applied her makeup in the rearview mirror as usual.

"How was practice?" she asked, puckering her lips in the mirror before shifting the SUV into gear.

"Good," Jimbo said, flipping some damp blond hair out of his face and turning toward Cory in the back. "What did you have? Seven touchdowns? Cory's killing it."

Cory blushed, liking it. "Well, you're the one who threw three touchdown passes. You're looking good too."

"It all looks good. B'ville better be ready for a spanking Saturday." Jimbo changed his mom's radio to some station and began to sing along. That left Cory looking out the window.

Cory's mind was on B'ville too, the big scrimmage where he'd either launch his career or stumble. He'd never played in a scrimmage where so much was on the line. Before all this, football had been a dream where he'd wished hard for a happy ending but never really got there. Even the game against the Cicero Falcons, where he'd gotten Coach McMahan's attention, had happened so fast and unexpectedly that it still didn't seem real. Saturday was real, though, and Saturday was what filled his mind when they pulled through the open gates and up into the circle.

Cory knew something was wrong before Mrs. Muiller cried, "What in the world . . . !"

The thing about the Muillers' mansion was that everything stayed in its place. Besides Helga, two cleaning women and at least three outdoor landscape workers combed the property inside and out, day after day. The whole thing made you want to wash your hands, brush your hair, and smooth in your shirt to fit in. It was as though anything out of place broke some unwritten rule.

When Cory saw the front door hanging wide open and the jagged glass of the broken window next to the door, his jaw dropped.

"What the—?" Jimbo opened his car door.

"You stay right here!" his mom snapped, while she got out herself. "Get back in the car and don't move."

Jimbo's mom had her cell phone out. She dialed quickly,

put the phone to her ear, and moved cautiously toward the front door. Somehow she sensed Jimbo's hesitation. She turned and pointed a finger at him. "In! And lock the doors. I'm calling the police."

That sent a jolt of fear through Cory, because why would she say that?

Jimbo, sensing from his mom's sharp tone the seriousness of whatever was going on, did as she said, and the door clunked shut.

"What happened?" Cory asked quietly in the silence.

"I have no idea," said Jimbo, eyes locked on his mom as she crept up the steps, talking again into the phone. Cory could hear him breathing.

Mrs. Muiller paused at the doorstep before she disappeared into the dark, open house.

"That's it." Jimbo flung open his door and started after her.

"Jimbo!" Cory ran after him.

They found her at the bottom of the stairs, peering up and speaking curtly into the phone. "They need to get here now if you don't want me to take matters into my own hands!"

"Mom, come on." Jimbo dragged his mom by the arm and convinced her to wait for the police with him and Cory on the steps.

It seemed like five years, but it was probably no more than five minutes before Cory heard a racing car engine. A police car rocketed into the circle and shuddered to a stop. In an instant, two policemen burst from the car with guns drawn. Cory made eye contact with the one first up the steps, but he might as well have been looking at crash test dummy. The cop's face was blank and serious and his eyes went right on past.

The police entered the house and everything went silent again.

When the police reappeared in the doorway, their guns were holstered. Jimbo and his mom stood beside them as they examined the door and the broken window without any apparent urgency.

Mrs. Muiller broke the silence.

"We were *robbed*." Jimbo's mom punctuated her words with a sob that ended as suddenly as it began. Cory wondered if she'd made the sound at all.

"It's actually a burglary," said one cop as he ran his fingers along the doorframe. "No one was home. No one threatened."

"Don't tell *me*." Her voice shattered with emotion. The tone startled them all, and both cops looked up at her from their work.

"They got at least a quarter-million dollars in jewelry from my dressing table drawer. At *least*." Her eyes widened as though she only now realized it. "Don't tell me I wasn't *robbed.*"

Her eyes swelled with tears, and one spilled down her cheek. She sniffed more of them back. The value of her jewels shocked Cory. He knew diamonds dripped from Mrs. Muiller's ears, wrist, and neck. He and Liam joked about it. Still—a quarter of a million dollars! He never imagined that she'd leave things worth that much money just lying around.

The offending policeman—his name tag said WELLS—looked at his partner, who put a hand on Mrs. Muiller's shoulder. "I know it's hard. Everyone thinks their home is safe."

"We have an alarm. What good did *that* do? Ha!" Her laugh was a bitter noise.

"It looks like it wasn't turned on." Officer Wells pointed at the keypad. He was a muscular man with dark stubble for hair and the hardened face of a wrestler.

"Oh, I turned it on all right." Mrs. Muiller put her hands on her hips and stepped up to the keypad. "I *always* put it on when Helga's gone."

"Who's Helga?" The other policeman, name tag BLANKENSHIP, had a notepad out.

"Our housekeeper," Mrs. Muiller said. "It's her day off."

"We'll want to speak with her," said Blankenship. "I presume she knows the code?"

Mrs. Muiller stopped and blinked. "Of course she knows the code. You're not trying to say Helga did this."

"Whoever did it knew the code." Officer Wells had been examining the broken window, and now he stood up. "It's a pretty clean job. They broke the glass, reached around, opened the door, and then—if you're sure the alarm was on—they disarmed it with the pass code. We're not saying it's your Helga, but maybe someone who got it from her. Lots of times you'll find a kid or a grandkid with a drug problem and they get it out of someone."

"Oh my God." Mrs. Muiller buried her face in her hands.

"Maybe you should sit down, ma'am." Officer Wells led her into the house. Immediately to the right of the entrance was an elegant room he pointed to. Cory had never seen anyone in that room, even though its walls were hung with fancy oil paintings in gold gilt frames that matched the furniture.

"No, we don't sit in that room," she said, heading through the house to the kitchen table, where they all sat down.

"Are the paintings in that room valuable?" asked Blankenship, pointing back toward the front door.

"Very," Mrs. Muiller said.

"So, they weren't professionals." Wells looked at Blankenship, then at Jimbo and Cory. "And, I assume your kids know the security code?"

"These are both your kids, right?" asked Officer Wells.

There was something in the policeman's tone that strangled Cory's stomach. The answer was no, he wasn't one of Mrs. Muiller's kids. Not really.

He was from the Westside. He was the scholarship kid.

"Jimbo is my son and Cory is staying with us." Mrs. Muiller gave Cory a worried look, like she hadn't even noticed he was there until now.

And the way everyone looked at him—even Jimbo—told him he was completely alone in all this. They thought he was somehow involved in the crime.

The officers took Cory into the TV room with its wood-paneled walls, old framed movie posters, and the thick, comfortable couch where the Muiller parents liked to sit and watch movies. The police put him on the couch and sat across from him in chairs they moved from the edges of the room. Blankenship slid the doors closed and they thumped together, sealing Cory off from the rest of the world.

At that moment, the thought of Cheyenne burst alive like a flame in the darkness. She was bold enough to barge right in, even on two policemen. She seemed to know him—really know him—better than anyone outside his mom, Liam, and maybe Gant. He was so hungry for her help he could taste it.

But he knew that on Thursdays Cheyenne went from soccer practice at school to skills practice with her travel team at the Mount Olympus Sports facility. So he sat on the edge of the couch, twisting his fingers together, and pleaded with his eyes so the police could see he had nothing to do with any of this. The questions he'd answered so far were a blur.

"Okay." Wells leaned forward and a vein in his forehead throbbed. "We hear what you're saying. You don't know anything about this, but you knew about the jewelry, right?"

"What do you mean?" Cory asked.

"The jewelry." Wells threw an impatient hand in the air. "You knew Mrs. Muiller has a lot of jewelry, right? I mean, you're not blind. The woman's got more bling than Kim Kardashian."

"I know she wears a lot of jewelry," Cory said, feeling it was a safe thing to admit.

"Just tell us the truth." Blankenship spoke with gentle understanding. He sat back in his chair, hands resting on his knees. "Everything is fine; we just need to sort it out so we can cross you off the list, Cory. Relax."

"She wears a lot of jewelry. Anyone can see that," Cory said firmly.

"Right, so you knew about the jewelry in her drawer," Wells continued.

"I know she wears jewelry, not where she keeps it."

"Well, you know it doesn't just appear on her like magic, right?"

"No." Cory felt like he was slipping on ice.

"So it had to be in her bedroom, right?"

"I guess."

"Is there another place she'd keep her jewelry?"

"I don't know." Cory looked to Blankenship, but the smile was gone.

"I don't know why you can't just say it, Cory."

"Say what?"

"That you knew the jewelry was in the bedroom."

"No one told me that."

"I get that, but they didn't have to." Wells glowered at him. "You said you knew she had jewelry and you said you didn't know anyplace but the bedroom, therefore it was in the bedroom and you knew it. That's all I'm saying. Am I right?"

Cory knew what was happening. He'd seen too many shows not to know that the police were suggesting things, manipulating him to say what they wanted. Still, he ignored the warnings in his mind because he hadn't done anything wrong and he wanted to show them that he was a good kid, so he swallowed and said, "Yes."

Wells suddenly got nice. "I mean, let's not play games, huh? If you know something, don't get cute. That won't help you. You're a good kid, but you come from a rough part of town, right?"

"Yes." Cory nodded; no question about that. He wanted to help. He didn't want to play games or be cute. That wasn't him at all, and he wanted Officer Wells to see that. Did he want to be a lawyer one day? He sure did, but now wasn't the time to play lawyer. This was serious.

"And you know the security code."

"I said that." Cory's throat got tight.

"Who did you share it with?"

Cory hesitated. He hadn't told anyone, but he knew his mom and Liam had heard him say the code when they left the Muillers, the night he met Marvin.

"No one," he said.

"No one?" Wells stared without blinking. "You seem unsure."

Cory clenched his teeth. His mom had nothing to do with this, that he knew as sure as he knew his name, so it wouldn't do any good to say that. He wasn't going to point a finger at Liam either. "I was just trying to think if I did, but I didn't."

"Really? That's the truth?" Officer Wells's voice mocked him.

Cory got mad and wondered if in fact he shouldn't be a bit more like a lawyer if these guys weren't going to believe him. "Yes. Why would I tell anyone?"

Wells stared at him for what seemed like ages before he spoke again. "What kind of trouble have you been in before?"

"No trouble," Cory blurted.

"Really?" Wells acted like that was a joke, like he knew something.

Cory suddenly remembered being a lookout for Dirty and Hoagie and Finn. He felt like he might fall off the couch. The room tilted as his mind spun back and forth, replaying the scene at the Shamrock Club with Officer Thorpe and Officer Kenny. They'd tried to scare him into talking, but he wasn't booked. He wasn't charged. So, from a technical, legal standpoint, it was like it never happened for Cory.

Cory shook his head.

"Speak up," Blankenstock ordered.

240

"No."

"No?" Wells looked like he'd taken an arrow in the gut.

"No." Cory exhaled, confident now and feeling better, even though he knew it was a lie.

He was lying to the police and suddenly his mother's voice wailed—a siren inside his head—telling him to take it back and tell the truth . . .

Before it was too late.

68

"So, we're not gonna find any kind of record of anything?" Wells did not believe him. That was obvious. "You're squeaky clean?"

"Yes." Cory nodded his head, because now he *was* telling the truth. There was no record.

Blankenship seemed to sense this and he stood up to go. "Okay, kid."

Wells looked up, surprised. "Really? You're buying this?"

"He's telling the truth." Blankenship frowned at his partner. "You know that?"

"C'mon, Pete. We got work to do." Blankenship broke open the doors.

Cory sat by himself, not knowing what to do next. He heard Mr. Muiller talking to the police at the front door and then his footsteps before the big man stood in the opening. "You okay?"

"Sure." Cory stood up and shifted on his feet.

"Police are paid to be suspicious," Mr. Muiller said. "Don't pay any attention. I told them no way did you have anything to do with this. I can read people pretty good, Cory. I didn't get to where I am without being a good judge of character. Come on. Let's go get Cheyenne and we'll have a plate of spaghetti at Angotti's."

"You're not . . ." Cory searched for the right word. "Mad? Upset?"

Mr. Muiller shrugged. "There's insurance. It's just jewelry. What gets me is that someone was in the house. That's what really burns me."

"Oh." That's all Cory could think to say.

"Hey, go get changed and we'll get some dinner. Sound good?" Mr. Muiller made everything seem normal.

Cory went downstairs to his room and put on a clean shirt. On his night table was the TracFone, and Cory fought himself before he gave in and picked it up. He wanted to be a man and deal with the problems life sent his way on his own, but if he could just hear his mom's voice, he felt like it would help. Mr. Muiller was nice, but there was nothing Cory could ever do that would make his mom turn her back on him. He needed to connect with her.

The phone rang three times before a voice said, "Hello?"

Cory's stomach turned and he hung up.

He hadn't called to connect with Marvin.

They loaded up the Bentley and drove to Mount Olympus Sports, everyone quiet. When Mrs. Muiller saw Cheyenne, she jumped out of the car and burst into fresh tears, hugging her daughter on the curb. "Oh, Cheyenne, we were robbed. The ring I always wanted to give you is *gone*."

Mr. Muiller rolled his eyes. "Deb, in the car, *please*. It happened. We're fine. I'll get you another ring."

Cory slid to the middle seat. Cheyenne got in, flushed but tired looking.

Jimbo leaned across the seat to Cheyenne. "Cops thought Cory helped rob the house."

"That is not even close to the truth, Jimbo." Mr. Muiller spun around in his big leather seat. "What's wrong with you?"

Anger flashed in Cheyenne's eyes. "*'You are not worth another word, else I'd call you a knave.'*"

"Well, they did." Jimbo sulked at his father before glaring at Cheyenne. "And stop talking like that, anyway. You sound like such a dork."

"You okay?" Cheyenne asked Cory in a low tone that shredded his heart.

"Yeah," Cory said, sounding as indifferent as he could. "The whole thing is crazy."

"We're over it and Cory is fine. Let's go get some pasta." Mr. Muiller put the car in gear and cruised away from the sports facility. He switched on the radio and listened to the news.

When a local reporter interviewed the mayor about the recent rise in crime, the mayor talked about the need for jobs, almost making it sound like it wasn't the fault of the criminals.

"Seriously?" Mrs. Muiller sputtered, pointing at the radio. "I wonder how she'd feel if she lost *her* rings. We need more police on the streets is what, and *she's* talking about jobs?"

Mr. Muiller switched the station to classical music, flooding the Bentley with tones as rich as the polished wood dashboard and leather seats. The food at Angotti's was delicious, but halfway through his plate of spaghetti and meatballs, Cory couldn't ignore the fact that Mrs. Muiller was acting strange, glancing at him between bites. He had to force himself to keep eating, like he was unconcerned.

Cheyenne and her father chatted pleasantly about how she was really bending the soccer ball into the corner of the net with consistency. Jimbo acted like all the fun and touchdowns of the past week hadn't happened. He glowered and sulked, bent over his plate of food like he thought Cory might take it.

By the time they got back to the house, Cory was convinced

that the Muiller family was solidly divided, Cheyenne and her dad for him, Jimbo and his mom against. Still, no one said anything about it. Cory did homework in his room and went to bed without the visit from Cheyenne he hoped for.

The next day at breakfast, things seemed somewhat back to normal. No one spoke about the burglary at the table. Cory wondered if he hadn't imagined the whole split-family thing, until Mrs. Muiller dropped them at the school and called Jimbo back to the car for a whispered conference.

Word of the robbery—even though it was technically a burglary—spread like wildfire through the school, and by lunch it seemed like the entire student body was split into the same two camps as the Muiller family: those who sneaked suspicious looks at Cory and those who smiled with sympathy.

Gant said, "Cory, stay strong. Only the strong survive."

To prove his point, Gant reached into his pocket and produced a single Mexican jumping bean. "See? This one's strong, so it lives on. I buried the other two. I don't know, maybe something will grow. A bean plant or something."

Cory studied Gant's face to see if he was serious and saw that he was. They were sitting at their usual lunch table with their free lunches, and Cory suddenly wasn't hungry. It sickened him that Mrs. Muiller could think he'd be involved in stealing from a family that was so generous to him.

"You gonna eat that?" Gant peered at Cory's tray; his own had been swept clean.

Cory pushed the chicken fingers Gant's way.

"You know who probably had something to do with it?"

246

Gant waggled his eyebrows.

"With what?"

"The robbery."

"It wasn't a robbery," Cory said. "That's when they wear a mask and carry a gun and say, 'Stick 'em up.'"

"Whatever." Gant stuffed a hunk of chicken into his mouth.

"Who?" Cory couldn't help asking.

Gant swallowed and leaned his way. "Mike Chester."

"What? Why would you even say that?" Cory couldn't keep the note of excitement out of his voice. Wouldn't it be wonderful if Mike somehow got the blame? He wasn't from the Westside, but he wasn't rich like the Muillers, either.

"This whole thing is messing you up, bro." Gant's thick eyebrows came together. "He wants that starting job. You choke in the scrimmage tomorrow and he's in."

Cory looked over at the table where Cheyenne sat with Tami and Tiffanae and the rest of the girls' soccer team. "Gant, whoever did this took like hundreds of thousands of dollars' worth of jewelry. It's a major crime. Mike's not going to do something like that just to mess me up so he can be the first-team running back. He could go to jail."

"I don't know. I'm trying to get you focused. We got a good offensive line and if Mike gets the starting job, it's not gonna be easy for you to replace him anytime soon. He's gonna run for a lot of yards. Coach P doesn't move things around once the season gets going."

Cory saw Cheyenne get up, toss her trash, and head his way with a smile that warmed him through and through, despite

247

everything. It raised Cory's spirits and his confidence. He said to Gant, "So, you know what *that* means?"

"What's it mean?" Gant asked.

Cory stood up to welcome Cheyenne with a smile before answering. "It means tomorrow's the biggest day of my life."

70

As they marched out onto the field to warm up for the scrimmage, the sky overhead darkened. B'ville was already there, decked out in red helmets and pants with white jerseys and looking huge. Cory looked to the top of the bleachers to find his mom. When he spotted Marvin sitting on the seat next to her, he dropped his hand, hardly knowing if he was angry or sad.

When thunder rumbled in the sky, the coaches shouted to each other and then their players. Both teams scrambled back up the hill and into the school gym while parents and fans took cover in their cars. There was an almost festive air to the whole thing, until the gym became a jungle swamp of sweat and heat. Then there was talk of canceling the scrimmage. Jimbo assured everyone that the forecast wouldn't allow them to play.

"Lightning all day," he announced. "Don't even know why Coach P tried."

Cory distracted himself by playing rock, paper, scissors with Garrison and Parker until he thought he'd lose his mind from boredom. He searched the crowded gym and found Gant tucked into a corner, fiddling with his jumping bean.

"Where'd you get that?" Cory sat down cross-legged beside him.

"It's my bean." Gant poked it and looked up from his palm. "But I think it died."

That disturbed Cory. He sat down next to his friend. "Well, you shouldn't be taking it into a live football scrimmage. Let me see."

"It was in my sock." Gant dumped the bean into Cory's hand. "For luck."

"You don't need luck," Cory scoffed. "You're a mountain." He cradled the bean in his palm. "Maybe this thing is just tired. You probably overheated it."

"Maybe," Gant said, taking it from him and slipping it back into his sock, "but that's the life of a jumping bean. You go where they put you and you better jump when it's time."

"What are you gonna do with it?"

Gant looked at the little lump in his sock. "I'll see. If I don't get any life out of it, I'll bury it with the others. If I get five pancakes, Mr. Trimble always gives me an Amazon gift card, and then I can order some more online."

"Online?"

"That's how the Trimbles get things. They have a Prime account, so it's free delivery."

250

Cory had overheard Cheyenne talking about buying books online, and Mrs. Muiller once said something about some shoes she called Prada, but it didn't go that way on the Westside. It was the Dollar General or a drive to Walmart for your stuff.

"Crazy, right?" Cory said.

Gant shrugged. "It works for them."

A whistle blast got everyone's attention. It was Coach P. "Okay, we are clear. Pads on and let's get out there!"

Both teams went into action. Tension joined the brotherhood of heat and sweat, and soon Cory's team was marching back down the blacktop path to the varsity field with an army of B'ville players close behind. Cory kept his eyes out of the stands. He'd worry about Marvin and his mom after the scrimmage. He glanced back at Mike and reset his mind.

This was it.

They warmed up quickly because both coaches wanted to get as much action in as they could before the weather sent them back inside. The sky remained an angry tangle of dark clouds that quietly spit rain on and off. It pattered against Cory's helmet. There were referees on hand and they conducted a coin toss, just like a real game. Jimbo went out and won the toss, selecting to take the ball.

"Offense, here we go!" Coach P bellowed.

Mike took the first series and didn't do anything special. He gained three yards on a sweep and got stuffed at the line on a dive play before Jimbo threw an incomplete pass. HBS had to punt. B'ville came out, threw a long pass, and scored on the first play. The HBS defense slumped off the field.

Coach P turned red and he bellowed at his offense. "I want

a *score* on this series! You hear me? We are gonna march down the field and tie this thing up and start over. Mike, let's go, son! Turn it on!"

Garrison Green took a short kickoff and plowed his way to midfield, giving HBS a boost. The offense went out and ran a toss sweep to Mike, who got hit behind the line and fumbled. The ball squirted from his hands and got lost in a pile of bodies. Referees peeled players away to find that B'ville had recovered.

Cory's rival jogged off the field with his head down. Coach P didn't even look at him.

The HBS defense swarmed onto the field, hooting and hollering, but the B'ville offense chewed them up, driving down the field to score another touchdown in seven plays.

Coach P's face turned purple and he spun around and grabbed Cory's face mask, pulling him close. "Okay, Marco Scholarship. This is your time. Don't let me down. I want to see that magic. I want a touchdown. I'm gonna feed you the rock until we score or punt. You score, you make my day and this competition is as good as over, but I want to *see it.*"

Cory swallowed.

"You got this?" Coach P looked like he might burst. "This is your chance, kid."

"Yes," Cory said. "I got this."

Coach P stomped off to roust up the kickoff return team.

This was *it*.

Cory tried to breathe deep in the huddle.

Jimbo called a forty-two dive.

"Wait!" Cory couldn't help from blurting out. "Forty-*two*? Jimbo, you sure forty-*two*? Not forty-eight?"

Jimbo scowled. "Forty-two dive on one, ready . . ."

The team broke the huddle. Cory tried to get Jimbo's ear. "It's just that they're killing us up the middle."

"Just do your thing, will ya?" Jimbo spun on him. "Everything's something with you. You know that?"

Cory bit into his mouthpiece and lined up beside Jimbo, who stood five yards behind the center in shotgun formation.

"Down! Blue eighty-nine, blue eighty-nine, set, hut!" Jimbo took the snap and tucked the ball into Cory's stomach.

Cory bolted toward the line, but it opened up like a razor cut. Red pants and helmets bled through. Cory lowered his shoulder and burst into it head on. Pads cracked. A white bolt of light flashed in his brain. His neck exploded with pain and still his legs churned forward, tearing up tufts of grass and dirt.

He tried to break free, but too many hands and arms snared his legs and he went down not much beyond the line of scrimmage.

Gant pulled him free from the tangle of limbs and propelled him toward the huddle.

"Why?" Cory asked. "Why up the middle? That's crazy."

"He knows what he's doin'," Gant said, surprising Cory. "Hang in there."

The next play, Cory faked the run up the middle so Jimbo could throw a play-action pass. Cory took the brunt of the defense so Jimbo could throw without pressure. He threw a good pass, too, but it bounced off the hands of the receiver and the HBS crowd groaned.

Third down and nine was a passing down, and the play called for three receivers to run deep routes. Cory was the checkdown, the safety valve in case no one else was open, the last resort.

"Chip the end on the right and get out to the flat," Jimbo told Cory as they approached the line. "I'm throwing it to you."

"Me?" Cory was confused. It wasn't that he didn't want the ball; it was that he wasn't supposed to be the primary receiver. Jimbo should have known that.

"Coach signaled for me to throw the checkdown."

"He did?"

"Stop talking and just do it, will you?" Jimbo got into his stance and began the cadence.

Cory didn't have time to think about the whys and hows. The ball was snapped and he chip-blocked the defensive end with his shoulder, spinning the defensive player off balance so the right tackle could bury him in the ground. He dashed to the flat, out near the sideline, turned, and there was the ball, whistling at him no more than eight feet away.

Cory's hands shot up, ready, and snagged the pass. He turned and saw open field. Two steps and the B'ville defense was coming at him from all sides. But this wasn't a run up the middle. This was where he could zig and zag, dip and rip.

He poured on the speed and crashed through a cornerback who thought he could tackle Cory high, then planted his hand in a safety's face, thrusting him into the ground. Cory leaped another tackler, dodged a fourth, and accelerated like a drag racing car, over the finish line, into the end zone under a light rain.

His teammates swarmed all over him, slapping his pads and palms.

"Touchdown Kid!" Gant hollered.

"Touchdown Kid!" shouted Jimbo.

"Touchdown Kid!" bellowed another.

On the sideline, Coach P hugged him, then let go. Cory flushed with pride and excitement. He looked up into the stands to point at his mom, and when Marvin gave him a thumbs-up, Cory gave him one right back.

It felt like he was on top of the world.

That's when someone tapped his shoulder and he turned around.

It was like a dream.

A bad dream.

Officer Wells stood dripping on the sideline in the middle of the HBS players, who were backing away like he was an infected zombie. Beside him was Officer Blankenship, looking angry to be out in the rain.

Officer Wells said, "Okay, kid. We know all about you and your Westside buddies. Come with us.

"Now."

Mr. Muiller was with the officers, huffing and wearing a dark blue rain coat and a matching floppy bucket hat. He seemed less in control than Cory had ever seen him. "Cory, let's just go with them and get this sorted out. I'll talk to Coach P."

It seemed to Cory that the entire crowd ignored the action on the field to stare down at him from the stands. Mr. Muiller took Coach P aside. Cory saw the coach glance his way and shake his head. Mr. Muiller returned, his mouth thin as a paper cut. Away they went, Cory surrounded by a triangle of adults.

Cory's mom and Marvin intercepted the four of them halfway to the parking lot.

"Excuse me!" his mom shouted, waving one hand and holding a newspaper over her head as a shield to the rain spilling from the smoky sky. "What in the world are you doing?"

Marvin followed close behind. Cory clenched his teeth.

Mr. Muiller stepped forward with his hands making calming gestures. "Ashley, I didn't know you were here."

"Of course I'm here," she said. "It's his first scrimmage."

"With the thunder and the confusion, I just didn't see you." Mr. Muiller was polite, but his voice had an edge to it now. "The police have some questions is all. Our house was broken into a few days ago. No one was hurt, but quite a bit of valuable jewelry was taken."

"You're his mother?" Wells asked, stepping forward.

"I am." Cory's mom stood straight, glaring.

"We just need to talk to him, ma'am." Blankenship stayed calm. "About the break-in. It was some kids he knows."

"Right now? Seriously?" She blinked her eyes and wore a look of disbelief. "He's playing football and you just take him?"

"Three hundred thousand dollars worth of jewelry was stolen." Wells looked grim. "And your son may have some information that can help us. I'd say that trumps a football scrimmage."

"I had no idea about any break-in." Cory's mom looked at Cory now like he'd done something wrong. She seemed to be losing control of the situation, if she'd ever had any to begin with.

Wells recapped the broken window, the deactivated alarm, and the value of the jewelry. "Kid we got is Albert Macadoo. They call him Dirty. We think he was involved in another burglary. A place called the Shamrock Club. We talked to some city cops who said your son was at the scene."

Blankenship took over. "But we don't care about any of

that. It sounds like Cory was an innocent bystander. We only want him to tell us as much as he can about these kids so we can catch the others."

"Are you saying he *has* to go? Now?" Cory's mom tried to sound tough, but she was weakening. He could tell.

"We can do this the easy way, or the hard way, ma'am," said Wells. "You can cooperate or we can go get a court order and bring him into juvie to see the judge."

"Well, I'm coming with you," Cory's mom said.

"That's fine, ma'am," said Blankenship. "Mr. Muiller? Would you still like to come anyway?"

"I feel like I should," said Mr. Muiller. "Can Cory ride with me or his mom?"

Cory could tell Wells didn't like that by the way the cop bit his lip.

"That's fine," said Blankenship.

Cory's mom looked at him. Cory flashed his eyes at Marvin. Suddenly he wasn't mad at the quiet man, he was embarrassed, so he said, "I'd better ride with Mr. Muiller."

They rode in silence until they pulled into the parking lot behind the police station, a three-story building next to the town offices. Mr. Muiller shut off the Bentley's engine and turned to Cory. "If you had a part in this, please just tell me now, Cory. I'll still help you, but I'd rather find out sooner than later."

Cory flinched. "No . . . Mr. Muiller, I didn't give anyone that code. I didn't do anything."

"But the police said you *know* these kids?"

Cory's mouth fell open, but nothing came out. His whole life was coming unraveled and it was so unfair because he'd done nothing wrong.

He didn't *know* Dirty. He just knew who he was and the kind of things he'd do. But he was very conscious of having lied to Wells and Blankenship before. Obviously they'd spoken with those policemen, Thorpe and Kenny.

"I know who they are, but I don't *know* them," Cory said finally.

Mr. Muiller looked at him for another moment, weighing things before a frown settled in. "Let's go inside."

They got out of the Bentley. The rain had stopped but drops beaded on the dark blue car like scattered jewels. Cory had a brief thought about the football scrimmage, wondering if Mike had been able to bounce back. He felt choked about his missed opportunity. Just when he'd tied the score and gotten the team back on track . . .

Cory's mom and Marvin hurried out of the Hyundai and joined them. They all followed the two officers inside and up the elevator. There were some chairs along the wall at the station. An empty desk guarded a door beyond.

Wells pointed to the chairs and addressed Cory's mom. "It'll be best if you all wait here so we can talk to Cory and Mr. Muiller."

"Shouldn't I be with him?" Cory's mom asked.

Wells didn't blink. "Ma'am, you made Mr. Muiller your

son's guardian so he could live in his house. I'm presuming you trust him."

"Of course I trust him." Cory's mom stiffened.

"Great." Wells pulled open the door. "Have a seat."

His mom looked uncertain. When she turned to see what Marvin thought, Cory bit his lip, then followed Wells through the door. He heard Blankenship say, "So, we're all set?"

From the other side of the door Cory heard his mom say, "Okay. I guess."

They walked along an interior wall with office doors to their right. To their left was a large open space filled with desks and bordered on the other side by floor-to-ceiling windows. They led Cory into a windowless room on the right. Wells pointed to a chair by itself on the far side of a table. Mr. Muiller took a seat on the end closest to Cory, but still far enough for Cory to realize he was alone.

Blankenship sat down across from Cory and crossed his arms.

Wells stayed on his feet. "Let's not mince words. You were the lookout in the Shamrock Club burglary for the same gang that broke into the Muillers' house, right?"

Cory looked at Mr. Muiller, who sat frowning. "I didn't do anything wrong. They made me."

"Did they make you help them this time, too? Or was it your idea?" Wells asked.

Cory was sick and spinning. He now thought it was a mistake to be in here without his mom. She knew about the Shamrock Club, but she understood. She knew how bad those kids were and that Cory had nothing to do with them. It seemed like he had slipped and kept slipping and now here he was with Mr. Muiller looking as unhappy as the police. "I had no idea about them doing this to the Muillers. I have no idea how or why."

"*How* was you giving them the security code," Wells said. "*Why* is because you saw all those diamonds around Mrs. Muiller's neck."

"That's crazy." Cory was sinking fast. They were bending what really happened and what he really said and he didn't know how to get them straight.

Then he realized he had a life preserver, something that would save him for sure, and he wondered why the police hadn't thought of it themselves.

It was so simple, Cory laughed out loud.

"This is *funny*?" Wells snarled.

"No," Cory said, knowing how they got the code.

All three of the men looked at him. "You better talk," Wells said.

Cory hesitated. What he was about to say would be disloyal. On the Westside, they'd call him a rat. But he wasn't on the Westside anymore, and he didn't want to go back. And things were the way they were. He didn't give anyone that code, but he knew who must have.

He needed to save himself.

Cory held back, trying desperately to think of another way, but knowing that there wasn't one.

The words echoed in his brain. "They must have gotten the code from Liam." But he couldn't say it.

Cory swallowed the bile juices churning up from his stomach.

Wells had a notebook out. He read from it and looked up, continuing. "You told us at the house that you knew Mrs. Muiller had all that jewelry. You knew where she kept it and you knew how valuable it was. That's what *you* said."

Blankenship nodded silently. Mr. Muiller's frown dropped even more. Cory couldn't speak. They were twisting things again.

"Cory." Blankenship opened his arms. "We don't want you in all this. We want Albert . . . Dirty. We want Finn and Hoagie.

We know all about them. We couldn't care less about you getting a slap on the wrist in family court, but them? They'll do time. They need to be put away. We just need you to help."

Silence smothered the room.

Cory couldn't allow himself to be connected to three thugs who were going to jail. He *wasn't* connected to them. He was a good kid. He'd never steal from anyone. His mother had taught him that.

"I don't know them. I know who they *are*, I said that, but I have nothing to do with them," Cory looked up, fierce. "Nothing."

Wells huffed and everyone turned toward him. "Cory, you know that's just not true."

Cory felt his insides knotting up, squirming like snakes in a bag. His eyes began to flood. "What do you mean?"

"We got a caller," Wells said. "Says you threatened Mike Chester with this Dirty kid in the locker room. Everyone heard you. You said he cuts people."

"I was . . ." The story was too big and too long. It flooded Cory's brain, drowning him while he watched the adults around him stare. He was a kid from the Westside. A scholarship kid like Gant, and Aidan Brown. Cory knew now what Gant meant. His shoulders slumped. He hung his head and went silent, defeated.

Mr. Muiller reached over and put a hand on Cory's shoulder. "Look, Cory. You come from a different world. We all know that. These kids . . . they probably threatened you, right? No one's saying you wanted to do this, but you've got to tell the truth and help these officers do their job."

Tears streamed down Cory's face. He sniffed and looked up at Mr. Muiller, who was trying to be kind to him.

Cory could barely speak, but he managed to sob out the words, "I *didn't*."

Mr. Muiller sighed heavily. "Officers, why don't I take him home. I think all this is too much for him, but I'm betting I can convince him to help, and then we'll call you."

"The problem, Mr. Muiller, is the jewelry," said Blankenship. "We got lucky to catch Albert—Dirty—trying to sell a ring, but the rest of it is out there, and every hour we wait is a chance for them to unload what they stole. Not every pawnbroker is as honest as the guy who called us with the ring."

"But tell me again why do you need Cory for *that*?" Mr. Muiller asked.

Blankenship said, "Like we said at the scrimmage, Mr. Muiller, Dirty won't admit he broke into your house. He's saying he won the ring in a card game. We know he's lying, but we can't prove it right now. Cory could help us nail them all. We could get warrants to search their homes, and once Dirty knows we've got Cory's statement, he may roll on his friends to save himself. So . . . we really need Cory to cooperate."

Wells spoke up. "I think he should stay right where he is until he talks. I say that with all due respect, Mr. Muiller, but this kid is a liar. He lied to us about never being in trouble before, and he lied to you just now about not knowing Dirty and not being connected to him."

Cory sniffed as quietly as he could. The tears continued to dribble down his face. He shook his head against the tide as Wells tried to take away any credibility Cory had with Mr. Muiller. He looked up and saw his host dad's face take on a deep scowl.

All Cory could do was silently plead, begging with his eyes for Mr. Muiller to give him a chance, even though no one believed him. He wasn't guilty.

Officer Wells drummed his fingertips on the table like raindrops from the end of the world.

Mr. Muiller stood up, shoulders back, with the upper lip on one side of his mouth raised off his teeth. "Come on, Cory. Let's go."

"Mr. Muiller?" Wells stared in disbelief.

"We're going." Mr. Muiller opened the door. "I don't like this. It's too much. He's a twelve-year-old kid."

The police were both on their feet now too. Cory stood up, eager to go.

"He helped break into your home, sir," Blankenship sputtered, "and steal your property."

"Cory's a good kid. This thing is a mess, but he's a good kid." Mr. Muiller ushered Cory out the door. "We'll sort this out at home and if I learn anything that can help you, I'll call. I've got your cards."

Wells followed them into the hallway. "Mr. Muiller, stop."

The urgency in the policeman's voice caused Mr. Muiller to pause and look back. Cory looked back too.

Wells wore a menacing smile. "As I told the mom, we can do this the hard way. I meant it. I'll bring him in front of a judge and we can put him into custody."

Mr. Muiller froze.

Cory had no idea what would happen next.

Mr. Muiller's face screwed up into a ferocious snarl, but his words were quiet and calm. "You know what I call your chief? Chief Stanton? Diggy. You never heard that before because only his close friends call him Diggy. Now, Officer Wells, I appreciate your passion for your job, but you can't bully me, son. I've got more lawyers than you've got spiders in your basement. I play in the big leagues and you'd do best to stand down, unless you'd like to explain all this to the Citizens' Police Review Board."

Mr. Muiller let Wells digest that before he said, "We good here?"

Wells swallowed and nodded.

"Nice. Like I said, I'll keep you posted if I learn anything." Mr. Muiller turned and put a hand on Cory's shoulder, guiding him under a firm grip out into the elevator lobby.

Cory's mom jumped up. "Cory, why are you crying? Why is he crying?"

"He's a little upset about all this." Mr. Muiller's voice was strong and calm. "But he's better now and we're going to get him home so we can talk. We're done here. I didn't like the way they were treating him."

"*You?* You brought him here!" Cory's mom raised her voice and she gave Mr. Muiller a vicious look.

"Mom, stop." Cory clenched his hands, begging, because this wonderful man had just pulled him from the jaws of a crazy policeman. "Just stop."

"I'm his mother," she said to Mr. Muiller.

"Ashley, please calm down. Of course you're his mother. Everything's going to be fine," said Mr. Muiller.

"I don't know how you can just say that." Cory's mom grabbed two handfuls of her long dark hair.

"I can say it because even if Cory is involved," Mr. Muiller said, "I'm the one who can shut this all down. I don't have to press charges."

"Cory's involved?" Horror iced his mother's whisper.

"Not in a foul way." Mr. Muiller pushed the elevator button. "They may have threatened him to get the code. I don't know."

Cory wanted to get the truth out, but more than that, he wanted to get away from the police station before something happened that trapped him in there again, so he stayed quiet. The elevator opened. Mr. Muiller hesitated, but when Cory stepped on, he followed, as did Cory's mom and Marvin. The elevator rumbled and plunged.

While they'd been inside the police station, the sky had begun to clear. Cory took the patches of blue between puffy white clouds as a sign, but as they walked out of the police station, Cory's mom caught up to him and put her arm around his shoulder. "Do you want to come home, Cory?"

"No." Cory spit the word out.

"Because of Marvin?" she asked, hurt. "Is that what this is all about? Why are you acting like this to me?"

"No. Stop, Mom." He shrugged free from her. "Mr. Muiller is gonna take care of things."

"You're twelve, Cory. I'm your mother." She looked like she might cry or scream, or both.

Cory shook his head and looked away. "No. I'm fine. Leave me alone."

"Fine." She spit the word at him and marched off, towing Marvin along by some unseen leash.

"Ashley, I'll call you with any news." Mr. Muiller raised his voice so she could hear, but if she did, she didn't give any sign of it.

She just kept walking.

Cory had never been so alone.

Mr. Muiller started the car and then turned to Cory. "Uh, the game's probably still going, but I doubt you want to go back there after all this, right?"

Cory shrugged. He couldn't imagine playing with everyone staring at him and his teammates distracted by the incident.

"Yeah, I don't blame you." Mr. Muiller put the car into gear and left the lot. "I wouldn't either. We can just get back to the house and relax."

When they reached the highway, Mr. Muiller said, "That was some touchdown you had, you and Jimbo. Heh heh! I mean, a short pass and you did most of the work, but it still goes down in the books as a touchdown *pass*, right? I love that."

Cory wanted to talk, wanted to act like Mr. Muiller, like everything was fine, but he couldn't manage anything more than a weak smile.

They went back to the house. The sky continued to clear, but Cory went to his room to read and think.

After a time, he heard voices outside his window. He pulled aside the shade and saw Jimbo with some teammates splashing in the pool. Sun now poured down through the trees. Cory watched. More kids arrived, Garrison, Mike, Parker, and Gant among them. Cheyenne appeared with Tami and Tiffanae, and she sat down on a deck chair beside Mike. Cory let the curtain drop and returned to the chair in the dark corner of his room. He picked up his book and tried to drown the noise of happy kids in the words of his book. No luck.

After some time, a knock on his door brought Mr. Muiller, dressed in a Hawaiian shirt and shorts. In his hand was a long spatula, a king's scepter. "Come on out. You're a part of the team, Cory. We won! And we wouldn't have won without your touchdown, you know. The score was 26–21."

Cory shrugged and held up his book like it would be a punishment to leave it. "I'm at a really good part."

Mr. Muiller looked at Cory and sighed. "You know, when I was a kid, we went camping at this place. They had a swimming hole in an old quarry, and you'd jump off this rock cliff into this emerald green water. They said it had no bottom, or not one anyone had ever been able to find."

Mr. Muiller put a hand on the top of the door frame and leaned into the room. "Scared the heck out of me. I wouldn't go in, hot as it was. My brothers, they all teased me the way brothers do, but no way was I jumping in. Then my dad said to me, he said, 'Son, your whole life you're gonna come across water and other things where you can't see the bottom, and if you can't jump in, you're gonna live a very dull, very average life.'"

Mr. Muiller smiled at Cory as if Cory knew what he meant, but Cory frowned and tilted his head.

Mr. Muiller kept smiling. "My dad knew I wanted to be anything but average, so, of course, I jumped. Loved it. I swear I can feel that water and the breeze and see the sparkle of the sunshine on those ripples.

"I know you're like that too," he continued, "like me. You're hungry. I see that quiet fire in your eyes. You want to do things, go places. That's why you're here. Not a lot of twelve-year-old kids just up and leave their homes. So, what I'm saying is, jump in. Put your book down and get out there. I know you can't see the bottom, but there's nothing out there that's gonna kill you. You can tell them I'm handling the police, that everything is fine, and to come talk to me if they have any more questions."

Mr. Muiller slapped the spatula against the open door a couple of times to get Cory's full attention. "Besides, Cheyenne is out there and she'll take care of you."

Cory swallowed and wondered if Mr. Muiller knew the effect Cheyenne had on him. He was as embarrassed as he was excited about the prospect of her being on his side.

"Yeah, I thought that'd tilt the balance," Mr. Muiller said, grinning. Then he disappeared.

Cory sat for a minute, thinking as the sounds of laughter and splashing sifted through the window.

He closed his book and took a deep breath before pulling on his bathing suit and heading outside. He let himself out through one of the glass doors off the game room and into the thick crowd of his teammates and girls' soccer players. It felt like deep water, murky and forbidding.

It was painfully obvious that everyone was looking but no one had a thing to say.

Cory couldn't go forward, but he couldn't go back either.

Cheyenne saw him and jumped up from her chair.

"Hey, Cory," she said, her blue eyes sparkling. She wore a tie-dyed cover-up shirt over her bathing suit with her long, blond hair pulled back into a ponytail. "We were just talking about you. My dad said everything worked out. You were doing so great in the scrimmage. Without you, B'ville would've smoked us. But it doesn't count, so everyone's just thinking about the opener next week and West Genesee."

Cheyenne spoke loud enough so that everyone could hear, setting the ground rules for the rest of them. Cory's feelings of embarrassment and excitement fought for control.

"What's that defense West Genny plays, Jimbo? What'd you call it?" She raised her voice above the noise.

Jimbo had half a cheeseburger in his mouth, but he managed to say, "A forty-six. It's an eight-man front."

"Yeah, so there's that." Cheyenne rolled her eyes and spoke to Cory like he was the only person on earth, even though she had to know everyone was watching. "Want a burger? Come on. I'm hungry."

She took his arm and led him along the pool and up the stairs. Looking back down at all the staring faces, she leaned close to Cory and, in her Shakespeare voice, whispered, *"'Hell is empty and all the devils are here.'"*

"Meaning?" Cory had to ask.

"People like to gossip," she said. "And getting hauled off by the police seems to bring out the worst in the HBS world. But don't worry, we got your back."

"Thank you."

Smoke poured from the grill where her father was busy cooking. Cory looked back at the forest of stares and picked out his rival's dejected face. Mike saw him looking, bit into his lower lip, and looked away. Gant met them at the top of the stairs and bumped fists with Cory.

"What's up, bro? All good?" Gant's attempt to sound casual was forced.

"All good," Cory said.

Gant stared at him for a moment before coming out of his daze. "Oh, great. Crazy thing. Cops. They get excited, right?"

"What do you mean?" Cory couldn't help asking.

"Just, them arresting you," Gant said. "Glad it's all cool."

"It is." Cheyenne shot a look at Gant.

"They didn't arrest me," Cory said to set the record straight.

"Oh . . . sorry. So, let's eat." Gant's famous smile returned and they lined up so Mr. Muiller could serve them.

Cory thought he saw Cheyenne's father give her a secret wink and whisper, "Thanks," as he slid a snapping hot burger onto her plate. Cory and Cheyenne and Gant loaded up their burgers with pickles and onions, lettuce and tomatoes, and weighed down their plates with scoops of potato salad and baked beans. They wrestled sodas free from a monster cooler filled with ice and sat at the big table under the roof. They had it all to themselves as most everyone else had already eaten.

Gant had three burgers stacked up. He laid potato chips on top of some onion and tomato and grinned at Cory. "A triple."

Before taking a bite of his, Cory turned to Cheyenne. "Thanks for doing this."

"Doing what?" Her blue eyes sparkled.

Cory sighed. "I know what everyone thinks."

"*The fool doth think he is wise, but the wise man knows himself to be a fool.*' Who cares what they think?" Cheyenne held her phone out for a selfie and leaned close to Cory. "Make a face. Snapchat."

Cory forced a smile and crossed his eyes. Cheyenne stuck out her tongue and snapped a picture, sending it out for the rest of the HBS world to see. Everyone followed Cheyenne, and Cory couldn't help feeling proud to have her arm around him. It warmed his insides to be treated like this special, because she believed in him, despite how bad things looked. They ate and chatted about how Cheyenne's soccer team would fare without their top goalie, who'd been lost for the season with a broken leg. Cory couldn't take his eyes off of Cheyenne, and he soaked up how pretty she was the way a stone warms in the midday heat.

The sun blinked through the trees and the air had begun to cool when Tiffanae appeared at the top of the stairs. "Cheyenne, I bet Garrison a pizza that you can do a one-and-a-half backflip off the board. Come show him."

Cheyenne laughed. "I want half. Pepperoni."

"You got it." Tiffanae giggled and shouted down at Garrison, "Get your wallet out! Here she comes!"

Gant and Cory watched Cheyenne go, but they both continued to sit. When Cory looked at his friend, he was disturbed to see such a sad face. "Why are you looking at me like that?"

Gant just shook his head, his thick eyebrows scrunched down low. "Just feel bad for you, bro."

"Gant, why?" Cory blinked and looked around, keeping his voice low. "What are you talking about?"

"All this? Everyone against you."

Cory snorted. "Gant, Mr. Muiller and Cheyenne are on my side. That's all I need. They *believe* me. Everyone else will come around. Heck, it was their house that got broken into."

Gant's frown drooped even more. "No, bro."

"'No, bro' what?" Cory leaned toward his friend, wanting to choke him.

Gant looked him in the eye. "The Muillers don't believe you, bro. They think you're in on it. I heard the parents talking."

"What?" Cory's face contorted. "What did they say?"

Gant seemed speechless. "Uh . . ."

Cory's heart froze and he leaned across the table, grabbing Gant's thick wrist and pulling him closer so he could whisper. "Gant, these people love me."

"Bro, my wrist." Gant pulled free. "They love you until they don't, Cor. You gotta be realistic."

"Stop talking in riddles. They love me until they don't?"

"They loved Aidan Brown. Then he got nabbed stealing and then the bad hammy and . . . boom! Kicked to the curb."

Cory looked back and saw Mr. Muiller surveying the pool area with a fancy beer in one hand before whispering to Gant, "What did they say?"

"Arguing, really," Gant said. "*She* wanted to press charges, but *he* said it's just the way you grew up and that it helped you as a football player—being a tough street kid and all that—and that you'd realize living with them that you didn't have to steal."

"I *didn't* steal." Cory hissed. "I am *not* a thief."

Cory could tell that even Gant didn't entirely believe him. "Look, I'm your friend. Friends stick together through thick and thin. I get it. It stinks to have everyone around you tapping away on their phone and all you've got is a jumping bean in your hand."

"Gant, stop it. I did *not* steal from the Muillers."

"You didn't, but your posse did. Cory, I'm not an idiot, and neither are the Muillers."

There was a whoop and a scream, then a splash and cheering. Cory looked down at the pool to see Cheyenne surface with a smile and pump her fist in the air.

"Cheyenne?" he said, as much to himself as to Gant. "Her too? She thinks I helped Dirty rob them?"

"Wake up; the crooks knew the *code*. But that's the great thing about the Muillers." Gant patted Cory's hand as he spoke. "They're rich, but they feel sorry for people who aren't. Well, Cheyenne and her dad anyway, and they pretty much run the show."

Gant looked hopeful that Cory understood.

"And Mike? Bro, he helped you big-time today." Gant angled his head down toward the pool. "That dog won't hunt. He played like he was blindfolded. See, Jimbo needs a run game. Everyone knows that. That's where me and you come in. We give him that run game and a championship and he's all-state and goes D-I, full ride and all that. All you got to do is carry the *rock*."

Cory grabbed the edge of the table as if he was in danger

of floating away. "Wait, you mean they think I helped Dirty break into their home, but they're *still* behind me because I can run the ball?"

"Coach McMahan is like a god, and word about what you did in practice got around too. Now all you need to do is light it up against West Genesee, show everyone you're the real deal—which I know you will because I'll be opening the holes for you, bro." Gant grinned and held out his giant fist for Cory to bump.

Cory held up his hand and touched knuckles in slow motion. His words came out like cold molasses. "You mean . . . everything for me . . . depends . . . on how I play next Saturday?"

Gant laughed and grinned and his head bobbed. "Yeah, pretty much."

"And what if I *don't* . . . light it up?"

Gant's face sank. "Well, that won't happen, bro."

"But if it did?" Cory felt like he was poking his own wound.

Gant curled his lower lip over his teeth and swiped it with the back of his tongue. "Well . . . if you choked, you mean?"

"Yeah, if I fell flat on my face, choked like a turkey."

Gant sighed. "All I can say then is . . . Aidan Brown."

Cory glanced over his shoulder and saw Mrs. Muiller standing next to her husband now. Each of them had a drink. They toasted something and took their sips as they surveyed the pool.

"You mean they'll just keep burning through kids like me and Aidan Brown until they find one who can make their son look good on the football field?" Cory didn't want to believe it.

"Hey, bro." Gant shrugged. "I'm not complaining, and you shouldn't either. It's their money. They can do whatever they want."

81

It was a strange week.

Cory's mom came and got him on Sunday. She took him to Green Lakes Park for the day, just the two of them. She tried twice to talk to him about the police and the burglary, but he clammed up and wouldn't say anything other than that everything was fine and that Mr. Muiller had it under control. After trying to talk to him for the first half hour, Cory's mom got as interested in her book as he was by his. He was reading *Ender's Game* and grateful for such a good distraction. The rest of the time they were together, but it was as if each of them was alone.

Finally, the sun dropped behind the trees. They picked up their blanket and towels, then had burgers at McDonald's before she dropped him off with a kiss. "I love you, Cory."

"Thanks, Mom." He leaned away and opened the car door.

"And I want you to know that whatever I do, I have to try and help you. Even if it makes a mess, I have to do it because you mean more to me than anything, than my own life . . ."

Cory thought she was talking about Marvin. Maybe she'd break up with him. How lonely would she be then? He shouldn't let her do it, but that's what he wanted, selfish as it was. Cory felt his insides melting, so he hurried out of her little, battered car before leaning in. "Love you too."

He closed the door and hurried up the steps without looking back. Her car buzzed and rattled down the drive.

School was awkward, and Cory kept his nose in his studies.

The team was tense because of the game coming up, and besides Parker wrapping Garrison's padlock in a six-inch ball of tape, there was no fooling around.

Mike and Cory split reps with the first-team offense in practice, and Cory felt like he had a decent week of practice. Neither Mr. nor Mrs. Muiller said a word to him about the police or the break-in, nor did Jimbo or Cheyenne.

It was as if everyone around him was waiting to see how Cory performed on Saturday, and he knew as certainly as he'd ever known anything that his future at HBS—and probably everywhere—depended on how he played. No one said so, but if he didn't play well, he knew the police would be turned loose on him like attack dogs. They'd tie him to the burglary, even though he was innocent, and run him out of HBS.

Saturday morning couldn't come soon enough, and finally, it came.

Cory woke at first light. He dressed and wandered upstairs and out onto the terrace overlooking the pool. A squirrel scattered seed as it leaped from the birdfeeder, escaping into the trees. The sun winked at Cory through their leaves. A chill filled the air. Cory pulled the hood up on his sweatshirt and sat down in a big, soft chair. He took his feet down off the ottoman when he heard the door behind him open. It was Cheyenne, dressed in her bulky soccer sweat suit and clutching herself against the cold.

"Freezing out here." She sat down next to him. "What are you doing?"

"Just thinking. What about you?" he asked. She'd been nice to him all week, but he couldn't help feeling like it was some job her father had given to her.

"Nervous, I guess." She stuffed her hands in the big front pocket. "We play Liverpool. They won the state last year."

"And without your goalie," Cory said.

She nodded. "Big day for you today too."

Cory shrugged. "I'll be fine."

"See?" She gave his shoulder a gentle slap, then returned her hand to its pocket. She hugged her knees and set her head down sideways on them. "You're cool. Two weeks ago you would've been nervous."

"I am nervous." He laughed. "But having everyone think you're a street thug does something to you."

"Cory, you grew up different from everyone here." Her words were soft pillows stuffed with understanding and kindness. "People get that."

He shook his head. No sense in trying to convince her he was innocent. He realized it didn't matter. Maybe one day he could. He'd like that.

"Did I say something wrong?" she asked.

"No. Why?"

"Just the way you were looking, like you were frustrated with me."

"You're the best thing about all this." Cory waved his arms around. "No, don't laugh. I mean it."

"Thank you, Cory. I like you."

Their eyes met and she sent a chill up the knobs of his spine with her look.

"I . . . like you." Cory wasn't sure if she knew how much he meant it, or if she meant the same thing. The word "like" was wider than a football field.

"I have a quote for you." She smiled.

"Shakespeare?"

"Who else?"

"Okay," he said.

"'*We know what we are, but know not what we may be.*' I love that, even though it came from Ophelia, who was totally out of her mind."

"That fits," he said. "Since I'm totally out of my mind."

She laughed and poked him before the door flung open and Jimbo spoiled their moment.

"Cory, you ready, dude?" Jimbo clapped his hands and huffed into them. "Perfect day for football, man."

Jimbo slapped Cory a high five.

"And soccer." Cheyenne stood up. "Which is the most pop-
ular sport on the planet."

"Maybe for girls," Jimbo said casually. "That sport is for
TWMs—those without muscles."

"Google George Elokobi, you meathead." Cheyenne started
toward the house. "He plays soccer in England and you only
wish you had his muscles. And in case you still can't read,
women are now eligible for military combat units, so once
again you've proven that *a fool doth think he is wise.*'"

"You can take your Shakespeare and flush it." Jimbo grinned
and pointed to himself with a thumb. "There's a reason men
rule the world."

That got her. Cheyenne threw up her hands with a growl
and slammed the door behind her.

Jimbo laughed to himself. "She's a mope, right?"

Cory just sighed.

"Oh, yeah," Jimbo said. "I forgot. Anyway, you ready?"

Cory stood up. "I am."

"Good; let's go eat." Jimbo snickered as Cory held the door
for him. "I mean, it's not like your life depends on playing well
or anything. Haha. Just kidding."

While Cory knew that Jimbo liked to kid, he also knew
Jimbo wasn't kidding now.

The locker room was quiet as an empty grave.

Cory pulled on his gear with trembling fingers and ragged breath. He was sitting with his helmet beside him in a long row of teammates like skydivers ready to jump.

Gant leaned into him with a nudge, whispering, "Hey, look."

Gant fished a finger into the top of his sock and scooped out a bean. "I wasn't gonna say anything, but look . . ."

In Gant's giant palm the bean sat, dead.

"What?" Cory was annoyed. Why would Gant pull out his destroyed jumping bean?

"No, watch," Gant whispered, holding his hand just beneath Cory's chin.

Cory watched for a full minute. Nothing.

"Gant, cut it out." Cory pushed his hand away.

"No, watch." Gant's whisper was urgent and he brought his hand back up into Cory's face. "I'm telling you."

Cory huffed but watched.

The bean quivered, then jumped and went still.

"See!" Gant's shout rang out against the empty tile walls.

Everyone stared.

Cory nodded and whispered, "Yes, I see."

For some reason, Cory's spirit soared. It was a sign. Gant didn't have to say it. Cory knew why he wanted him to know that the bean was still alive, still kicking. He grinned at Gant and the two of them bumped fists with everyone else looking at them like they were two fools.

The door burst open, slamming into the lockers.

Coach P gave his whistle a blast. "Okay, you cupcakes! Let's get to business!"

With a war cry they leaped to their feet and streamed out of the locker room. They gathered in military columns outside the school and marched down the hill to the varsity stadium with its towering lights and bright green artificial grass. The stands weren't full, but there were plenty of people, enough to make some noise as the team jogged out onto the field to warm up. Cory saw his mom at the top of the bleachers, off by herself with Marvin by her side. He tried to ignore that and focus on his assignments.

West Genesee arrived and took the other end of the field, wearing white jerseys and gold pants that matched their helmets. They looked big and they chanted like Viking warriors, low and intense. Cory's stomach began to crawl with nerves. Twice, he thought he'd lose his breakfast, but he somehow got through warm-ups and "The Star-Spangled Banner" before Jimbo and Garrison marched out for the coin toss. Puffy clouds filled the blue sky. A cool breeze tugged at Cory's hair, but when the sun poked its face out, the temperature was perfect.

They won the toss and Cory put his helmet on, breathing deep. The kickoff return team swarmed the field.

Coach P grabbed him by the shoulder pad and thrust him into a loose huddle with the rest of the offensive players. "You start us off, Cory. Let's see something. Got it?"

The whistle blew. The ball sailed end over end. An HBS player muffed it and fell down on the ball amid a crowd of bodies, but HBS retained possession.

Cory hustled out, noise in his helmet like ocean surf.

Coach P was shouting from the sideline. Cory looked and raised both hands questioningly until he realized Coach P was yelling at Jimbo, something about the safety. Jimbo called the play, a toss sweep. Gant grunted. "Let's do this, bros!"

They lined up and Cory surveyed the West Genny defense. In the center of it all was a muscle-bound middle linebacker with a neck like a fire hydrant. His skin glistened with sweat and the red mouthpiece he wore made it look like he'd been chewing on a hunk of raw meat. Dark eyes peered out from behind the mask, sparkling with ferocious insanity. He wore number 56.

The linebacker paced back and forth as though caged in the space of grass across from Cory, and then he pointed. "Hey, Marco! Comin' at *you*, chump! Yeah, you! Gonna make you *hurt*! You ain't stealin' no win from us. Even though I know you're good at *stealin'*."

Before Cory could think or speak, Jimbo began his cadence and took the snap. Cory bolted from his stance and snatched the tossed football from the air without breaking stride. His wide receiver had a solid block on the cornerback and the tight end chopped down the outside linebacker. Cory poured on the speed, knowing a big gain waited for him right up the sideline and he'd shut number 56 up good with a touchdown on the first play.

Whatever hit him, hit him so hard he saw stars.

Yelling and dancing and hooting and nasty laughter rained down on Cory. He blinked up at a blue patch of sky and then saw arms waving and number 56 smiling around that red mouthpiece.

"Your lights out, Chicken Little? The sky fall on you? Hahaha!"

Gant appeared and shoved number 56. All that did was rile up the officials and make number 56 laugh louder.

"I told him so! I *told* you I was comin'. Can't be more fair than that! Not like I'm sneakin' around like no burglar. Hahaha!"

Jimbo helped Cory sit up and to his feet.

"An' I'm comin' *again*!" Number 56 grabbed his own face mask and jerked it straight, then laughed some more and stomped off. "So buckle up!"

"That's enough jabbering!" An official reached for his flag. "Unless you want a fifteen-yard penalty . . ."

Another ref put his hands on either side of Cory's helmet. "You okay, son?"

"Yeah," Cory said. "I'm fine."

"Good," said the ref. "That was some hit."

Cory grunted and hustled back into the huddle.

"What was that?" he asked Gant. "He said something about the burglary."

"All that social media stuff, bro. People talk." Gant shrugged. "Don't let him get inside your head."

The next play was a pass. Cory's job was to release up through the line and run an out pattern. The ball was snapped and he took off. When he dashed between two linemen, he took two more steps before number 56 knocked him off his feet with a crushing blow. He was so busy laughing at Cory, he neglected the wide receiver sprinting across the middle of the field to catch Jimbo's pass for a first down.

Number 56 wasn't bothered by the first down. He hovered over Cory and muttered so the refs couldn't hear him. "All game. All game. Comin' for *you*, Marco. Make you my *girlfriend.*"

Gant appeared and helped Cory up. Gant was furious. "What'd he say? What did he just say?"

"I must have broken his back in another life or something." Cory shook his head. "He's crazy."

"I'll show him crazy." Gant snarled and made two fists.

"That was no tackle. He's headhunting *my* running back? *My* bro? Jawing at you? Uh-uh. That don't happen. Not with Gant it don't."

"What are you gonna do?" Cory looked over his shoulder and saw number 56 pointing at him and nodding his head.

Gant yanked Cory toward the huddle. "You just watch the Gant."

The next play was a fullback dive behind Gant.

Cory faked a toss sweep but kept his eyes on his giant friend. Gant left the lineman in front of them unblocked, zipped past him, and charged number 56 like a mad bull. Gant hit him so hard he flew through the air, arms pinwheeling, until he crashed onto his back. The man Gant was supposed to block blasted Garrison Green at the same time and the whistle blew.

Cory darted to stop Gant, who hovered over the top of number 56. "It's on! You and me and that's just the first taste!"

The ref got to Gant first and pushed him back. Cory grabbed Gant's arm and kept him going toward the huddle.

From the sideline, Coach P screamed a red-faced scream. "*Gant!* You blocked the wrong man!"

Gant chuckled and talked under his breath. "No I didn't."

Jimbo knelt in the huddle and called the play, a short swing pass away from Gant.

"Perfect." Gant slapped his helmet twice and looked hard at Cory. "Catch the pass and cut it back, like a reverse."

"Gant," Jimbo snapped, "you're not running this offense."

Gant leaned into the huddle and glared down at Jimbo. "Shut your piehole, Jimbo. You want another touchdown pass, don't you?"

Everyone went silent.

Jimbo finally muttered something and called the play again as if nothing had happened before he broke the huddle. Gant grabbed Cory by the arm as they marched to the line. "Do what I said. Cut it back my way and take it to the house, bro. *I* got 56."

They all lined up.

The West Genesee middle linebacker scowled at Cory, but he wasn't jawing.

The ball was snapped. Cory took off to the sideline, turned and snatched up Jimbo's pass, and then turned back hard, reversing field and running for the opposite sideline. From the corner of his eye he saw number 56 rocketing toward him, chasing him down like a Discovery Channel cheetah on an antelope.

Gant appeared from nowhere and destroyed the middle linebacker. Cory burst forward and juked a cornerback. He accelerated, lowered a shoulder, and blasted through the strong safety. A linebacker hit him and he spun, falling, but caught himself with one hand before taking off again. The far-side cornerback had the angle to cut him off from the end zone.

Cory had plenty of time and he threw a perfect stiff-arm, guiding the cornerback's face into the turf as he sidestepped and surged into the end zone.

His team sprinted to the goal line and buried him in hugs and backslaps.

Cory was back.

And that meant HBS was back.

85

There was another touchdown pass on a screen from Jimbo, and two touchdown runs added onto that—four touchdowns in all for the Touchdown Kid. He tore it up.

Jimbo threw for four total touchdowns against a haggard and depleted West Genny defense, and HBS's crosstown opponent only put thirteen points of their own on the board to HBS's forty-six. The sideline was like a pool party, with guys joking and laughing and everyone getting some licks in on the other team out on the field. Only Mike Chester wore the face of a boy who'd failed a big exam. After the final whistle, Mr. Muiller climbed right over the fence and marched onto the sideline to grab Jimbo and raise him in the air.

Coach P looked on with a proud glow.

"I know where there's a barbecue with some thick cowboy steaks waiting to happen for a certain sixth-grade team," Mr.

Muiller announced to the tune of thirty-something cheers.

As the team lined up to shake hands, Mr. Muiller turned to Cory and hugged him tight, pulling his sweaty-wet head against a soft polo shirt. "You were spectacular, Cory. I believed in you and you made me so proud."

"Thank you." Cory felt comforted by the strength of the big man's hands.

Mr. Muiller raised Cory's face and looked down into his eyes with an intensity that bordered on scary. "I don't care what happened with all that break-in nonsense, Cory. I'm behind you. No matter what. You got that?"

"Yes, sir." Cory grinned and joined his team.

It finally felt like home.

86

Cory changed into jeans and a T-shirt in the locker room and headed outside with Jimbo and Gant. Jimbo played them a merry tune with fart noises, flapping his arm with the other hand in his armpit. The three of them were laughing when they burst through the door. Cory wasn't surprised to see his mom standing with the Trimbles and the Muillers, but his laughter faded away at the sight of Marvin's big round face. Before anyone could say a word, Cory's mom stepped forward.

"Great game, Cory." She hugged him quickly, then took his shoulders in her hands. "I know you want to celebrate, but first, I need to take you someplace."

"Mom, why? Where?" Cory looked at Mr. Muiller, but Jimbo's dad only shrugged.

"It's a surprise, Cory. You have to come." Cory's mom took

his hand and held it tight while she said good-bye to the other adults.

"Please join us for the barbecue. It's at the Trimbles', but you're more than welcome," Mr. Muiller said, nodding toward Marvin. "Both of you."

"Thank you." Cory's mom gave no indication of whether she planned to go or not, and she dragged Cory toward her car while his new friends and family watched.

"Mom." He spoke under his breath and tried to shake free from her grip without making a scene. "Where are we going?"

"Get in." She opened the rear door, but Marvin stepped forward.

"Why don't you let the star player ride in front with you?" Marvin slipped into the back seat, sliding in sideways to allow his large frame to sit.

Cory stood frozen for a moment while his mom gave him an I-told-you-so smile.

"Thanks, Marvin," Cory said, meaning it, and he got in front.

"You embarrassed me," Cory told his mom before looking back past Marvin and out the rear window to see everyone staring as they pulled away.

"This is important, Cory. You'll understand when we get there."

"Get where?"

His mom glanced over at him with an unbending face. "You'll see."

Cory had no idea where they were going, because they might have been headed back to the Westside or they might have been headed to the mall or a restaurant as they drove down Erie Boulevard. When they pulled into the town police station, his heart nearly stopped.

"What are we doing here?" Cory was frightened and sickened in equal measures. "Mom?"

"You'll see." His mom's face told no secrets. "It's nothing bad."

"Nothing bad? How could this be *good*?" Cory's voice rose to a frantic pitch.

"You'll see. Calm down." She stopped the car and got out.

Cory looked back at Marvin, who said, "It'll be okay, Cory. Trust your mom."

"Come on." She sounded like she was coaxing a dog into

the pound, but he couldn't help following. He wished he'd never left the safety of Mr. Muiller.

In they went and up the elevator. When they stepped off, Cory met the evil stare of Liam's mom. She smelled like wet cigarette smoke. Her face was puffy, and her eyes were red and moist.

She turned her glare on Cory's mom and muttered, "Witch."

Cory could see his mom was flustered, but she marched past Liam and Finn's mom with her head held high and addressed the woman officer sitting at the desk. "Please tell Officer Blankenship that the Marcos are here."

Liam's mom began to cough and hack. Cory didn't know if it was a response to his last name or just too much smoking.

Cory and Marvin and his mom waited just a few minutes, standing by the desk in the hate-filled silence before Officer Blankenship appeared and hustled them inside.

"Sorry about that," the tall cop said as he showed them through the open office area along a wall of doors. "It's been a busy morning."

They passed the interview room Cory had been in. The door was slightly open and Officer Blankenship quickly pulled it shut.

As it closed, Cory's eyes soaked in the scene. Inside, sitting with his back to the door, Cory recognized the short hair and thick shoulders of Officer Wells. Across the table in his wheelchair sat Liam, puffy-faced like his mom, tears streaming down his cheeks. His best friend was sobbing.

Cory stopped and his mouth dropped. The snap of the lock echoed in Cory's brain. Sickened, he blinked and grabbed his mother's arm. "Wait, that's Liam."

"Come *on*, Cory," Cory's mom insisted.

Cory trailed after her in a daze. Blankenship led them through the open space filled with desks and file cabinets into what looked like his private office, with a window behind a desk with several chairs. "Sit down and I'll be right back."

Cory sat, bewildered, and stared at his mom.

She beamed at him with pride. "I *knew* you didn't do it, Cory."

Cory looked at Marvin, who said, "Your mom remembered you telling her the security code in front of Liam and, man, she just went to work."

Cory's mom took an excited breath. "Did you know— of course you didn't—but they caught the Hogan kid on Wednesday and he spilled his guts. Told the police Finn had the four-four-four-four code. Finn also had a *gun*. I don't understand it, but that makes the whole thing a Class A violent felony, Cory. Those boys are going to *jail*. If you'd been a part of it—and even just giving them the code *makes* you part of it—you could have been sent to Hillbrook, and I was *not* going to let that happen. Especially because I knew it *had* to be Liam who told Finn.

"Remember at the barbecue? Mr. Muiller said the code *right in front of Liam*. I told the police that. I told them it wasn't *you*, it was *Liam*."

Cory's mind and insides were churning. "So why did you bring me here?"

"You'll see," his mom said.

Just then, the door opened and in walked Officer Wells along with Officer Blankenship.

Wells looked as mean and hard as ever. He glanced at Cory's mom, who frowned and tilted her head at Cory.

When Wells spoke, his voice had lost its edge. He sounded almost tired. "Cory, your mom wanted us to apologize to you, and she's right. I'm sorry. We were rough on you and we were wrong."

"Yes," Blankenship added, "I'm sorry too."

Wells looked at Cory. Cory couldn't speak, but he nodded that he understood.

Wells then looked at Cory's mom, all business again. "All set?"

Cory's mom allowed herself a small smile. "Yes. Thank you, Officer Wells. I think that was important for you to say and Cory to hear."

Wells nodded and opened the door. "Good, then I'll get back to my case."

Cory's mom and Marvin stood up. Cory did the same, and Blankenship held the door before leading them back toward the front desk. Cory followed the adults with his head hung low. When they passed the interrogation room where Liam was, Cory could hear the roar of Officer Wells's voice through the wall. His legs felt like sandbags, but he forced his feet to go, one step in front of the other.

When he reached the main doorway leading out, Blankenship held the door once again. The lobby was empty except for the officer at the desk. Liam's mom was nowhere in sight. Cory took one step into the lobby, then froze.

His mom reached the elevators and turned to look back at him. "Cory?"

"No." Cory shook his head and bolted back inside.

Cory burst into the room where Wells and Liam sat facing each other across the metal table.

His old friend sat with his face in his hands, trembling and sobbing softly.

"Liam?" Cory darted around the table and put a hand on his friend's shoulder.

Liam looked up in disbelief.

Wells jumped to his feet. "You can't—"

Cory's mom and Marvin and Blankenship appeared.

"Cory!" his mom shouted.

Liam gave Cory a pitiful look and sobbed, "They said *Hillbrook* . . ."

"No, you're not." Cory glared at the four adults. "He's *not* going to Hillbrook. He didn't do anything."

"He gave them the code," Wells snarled. "He's part of it. That's the law."

Wells spun around toward his partner. "I told you this was a bad idea . . . apologize?"

"That's *not* the law!" Cory's shout left everyone stunned and silent.

He gathered himself and spoke calmly. "Liam never *intended* for his brother to hear the code. *Intent* is an essential element of a crime. This is as much my fault as Liam's. We were joking about it—the code—over the phone, how silly it is, four fours. Finn must have *overheard* us. Liam isn't guilty of anything."

Cory pulled a chair out from the table and sat down. "If he's guilty, then I'm guilty too."

"Let's not get excited." Blankenship held his hands up in the air. "We just need Liam to tell us where his brother is."

"He doesn't have to tell you anything." Cory felt like he was outside his own body, listening to some other twelve-year-old kid tell the police what was what, but the kid was right. "Did you read him his rights yet? Is he even under arrest?"

The policemen's eyes met. Wells's look said "I told you so" to his partner.

Blankenship cleared his throat. "No, he is not under arrest."

"Then he can go, right?" Cory said.

Wells clenched his teeth and his jaw rippled with muscles beneath a red face. He glared at Blankenship like it was his partner's fault for being soft and agreeing to bring Cory in to apologize.

"I don't think that's a good idea," Blankenship said.

"Why?" Cory tried to keep his voice from trembling, even

310

though his hands quivered like leaves beneath the table.

"So, Liam is free to go with us?" Cory's mom asked. "That's how it seems here."

Blankenship looked at the floor and spoke through a tight mouth. "Yes. He is."

Cory's mom circled the table and put her hands on both boys' backs. "Let's go, kids. With all due respect, officers, we're done here."

90

The next Saturday, Cory ran for five touchdowns and the HBS sixth-grade team rolled over Rome Free Academy by a score of 61–7.

The bus ride back was full of fun. Laughter washed over them, back and forth like an ocean tide, unending and punctuated by farting noses and secret imitations of Coach P. When they piled off the bus, Cory's mom was waiting along with Marvin and the Muillers and Trimbles. Cheyenne was there too. Cory waved and marched inside to shed his gear for street clothes. Back out they went, receiving kisses and hugs like soldiers returned from battle.

The Trimbles had a party tent set up on the broad lawn beside their pool. Smoke poured from a Dinosaur Bar-B-Que catering truck with its own massive grill in tow. There was a DJ and a dance floor, and Cory couldn't help grinning up at his mom as they walked inside hand in hand and everyone broke into cheers. Mr. Muiller jumped up from his seat and raised Cory's arm like a heavyweight champ.

"Ladies and gentlemen," Mr. Muiller shouted, "the Touchdown Kid!"

Cory's mom and Marvin sat at a big round table with the Muillers. Cheyenne winked at Cory, got up, and waved him toward the buffet line. Cory rose from his seat, but Gant pulled him aside, shouting in his ear above the music.

"Can you believe this place?" Gant chuckled. "It's like a wedding or something. Big time, right?"

Cory looked around at the billowing white tent. Through a small vent hole above shone the bright blue sky. "No, Gant. It's better than big time. It's a dream come true. The only thing missing is Liam."

"Yeah, but he'll be with us too, soon," Gant said. "Time flies when you're havin' fun. Kids I know in high school say middle school's a blink."

"I just hope he keeps getting better," Cory said, raising his voice above the music. "Then they'll have to give him one of those ninth-grade scholarships."

"Well, you keep doing what you're doing," Gant shouted, "and then you'll just *tell* them to give your homeboy a scholarship."

Cory laughed and looked at his new friend to see that he was serious. "I'm gonna just *tell* them?"

Gant laughed too. "Yeah. You're gonna get whatever you want around here. You heard Mr. Muiller. . . .

"You're the Touchdown Kid!"